Master *of* None

Master *of* None

How a Jack-of-All-Trades Can Still Reach the Top

CLIFFORD HUDSON

HARPER
BUSINESS

An Imprint of HarperCollins*Publishers*

Mention of specific companies, organizations, or authorities in this book does not imply endorsement by the author or publisher, nor does mention of specific companies, organizations, or authorities imply that they endorse this book, its author, or the publisher.

HarperCollins books may be purchased for educational, business, or sales promotional use. For information, please email the Special Markets Department at SPsales@harpercollins.com.

FIRST EDITION

Library of Congress Cataloging-in-Publication Data

Names: Hudson, Clifford, author.
Title: Master of none : how a Jack-of-all-trades can still reach the top / Clifford Hudson.
Description: First edition. | New York : Harper Business, 2020. | Includes bibliographical references and index. |
Identifiers: LCCN 2020014400 (print) | LCCN 2020014401 (ebook) | ISBN 9780062889034 (hardcover) | ISBN 9780062889041 (ebook)
Subjects: LCSH: Hudson, Clifford. | Success in business. | Leadership. | Career development.
Classification: LCC HF5386 .H896 2020 (print) | LCC HF5386 (ebook) | DDC 650.1--dc23
LC record available at https://lccn.loc.gov/2020014400
LC ebook record available at https://lccn.loc.gov/2020014401

---

20 21 22 23 24 LSC 10 9 8 7 6 5 4 3 2 1

Contents

Master *of* None

Introduction

I don't believe I've ever had the patience to master anything.

Have you?

While the thrill of being perceived as an expert is attractive, the way I see it, life's too short and too fascinating to focus on one area for too long. There are too many other things to see, do, and be.

Plus, I imagine it gets plain boring staring down the same path every day. I wouldn't know from experience, though—I've always been a bit all over the map. It's the main reason I arrived at the helm of Sonic, a public, multibillion-dollar company that serves 3 million customers daily.

Frankly, getting there was one unplanned journey—I was handed the job in the midst of boardroom shock when my predecessor quit mid-meeting and said, "There's a plane waiting to take me to my new job." While I might have been considered next in line by some, I hadn't ever planned to be a CEO of Sonic or any other company. But the position was offered to me right then and there, and I said, "Sure, why not." (Truth was, there were plenty of reasons why not, but none were more compelling than a new experience.)

Staying in the position I was given for more than two decades was another unplanned journey. You can't really plan what you never saw coming. But the reality is that both getting there and staying there for the length of time that I did was the result of a fondness for variety and a continuously extending curiosity. Some might not consider my approach a legitimate strategy. They might even call it being easily distracted, impulsive, or preoccupied. I call it being versatile. It really doesn't matter what you call it—the results speak for themselves. As you'll see in the pages to come, there's been no shortage of adventure, opportunity, or enjoyment in my life. The business returns haven't been too bad either.

I wasn't anything special as a kid so I can't say I saw my career coming. Maybe you can relate. I was raised in Wichita Falls, Texas, which is equidistant from Oklahoma City to the north and Dallas (where I was born) to the south. It wasn't a town known for anything, and even today it shares features with the Midwest, South, and Southwest. That's another way of saying it was a typically indistinct American town and my family fit in. I was the little brother of four siblings, with one older brother and two sisters, one of them my twin, three minutes older than me. In our first house that I can recall, my brother and I shared a bedroom above the living room that was accessed via a narrow staircase flanked by high walls. It was the attic disguised as a bedroom—the only room those stairs led to, and back then I never considered it odd that we ascended into a dark windowless box to sleep. However, climbing those stairs each night and peering down them into the house below each morning is all I remember about that house. It is also my earliest memory. I was three or four when we moved across town. The image of that narrow staircase into the ceiling and that view from the top stuck in my mind—I can still see them today—which has led me to conclude that there was something about the staircase that piqued my young instincts.

At our new home, some early scenes have also remained stuck in my mind. The first is of me sitting outside our house on a sunny spring morning. My siblings were at school and I was playing on the white gravel between our driveway and front yard while my mom tidied up inside. As I rolled my small toy car over the rocks, the milkman pulled up to our curb. I watched intently as he retrieved a metal basket holding two glass bottles from his truck and delivered them to our back door, just off the kitchen, but in the carport. To this day, I can still feel the rising sun warming my neck and the thrill of being alone outside and the curious appearance of the milkman. There was a new world outside our home that I'd never imagined before.

The second scene that sticks with me is of my first fistfight. I was four years old and a boy my age who lived at the end of our block had decided to duke it out with me for reasons that are still a mystery to me (back then it seemed you didn't need a reason beyond proving yourself tough).

I wasn't going down without a defense. Fists flew in dog-paddle fashion until I got him and his flailing arms pinned to the ground. That's when he somehow managed to stretch his neck enough to reach my butt . . . with his teeth. He clamped down like a small, angry mutt. I can still remember being unable to sit down in the back seat of my mother's old Chevrolet that afternoon. Fortunately, I was still small enough to stand on the floorboard and hold tight to the front seat. One might say that boy was my first real pain in the ass. If anything, he taught me that not everyone is agreeable.

Another memory was my mother's pursuit of incremental financial support for our family. She sang beautifully and was known for her voice but had detoured her academic and musical careers to raise four kids. When my twin, Beth, and I were somewhere around four years old, our mother would take us with her downtown to a Wichita Falls funeral home, slide in a back door, put on a robe, ask us to sit quietly, and, at just the right moment, slip across the hall to anonymously sing at some soul's last service for a nominal fee. She would then quickly collect us and her cash, and we were on our way.

A psychologist could probably tell you what those memories mean, but as far as I know they paint a fairly clear picture of my early life. I enjoyed independence, mystery, and new discoveries and as a result was constantly involved in a smorgasbord of activities that didn't fit any particular pattern. I enjoyed sports and singing in the church choir. I socialized a lot, but also sat alone with a book quite often. I got into an inordinate number of fistfights through junior high, due less to my temperament than my convictions and the general culture of fighting at our school. I then spent my high school years uniting schoolmates through student government positions.

I wasn't an eccentric kid. I was just a curious one who seemed to lack any sense that I was supposed to choose a path or focus. My parents didn't make me. My teachers never taught me to or, if they did, I wasn't listening. I suppose I was never told I should have a "supposed to." Of course, like you and every other kid, I thought about what I wanted to be when I grew up—professional baseball player, politician, famous musician. There was just never any pressure to decide.

Instead, I was left to the one device that was most effective at getting me what I wanted: variety. Multiple pursuits kept things interesting and earned me storytelling credibility, a couple of good girlfriends, and a diverse group of comrades—black, brown, and white, jocks, band buddies, nerds, and leaders.

There were narrow, focused, and life-changing days too, like when I was eleven years old and learned of my parents' bankruptcy and felt the unwelcome upheaval for our family life that followed. I was later told that my father's business partner had embezzled funds from their company in order to support the lifestyle of his mistress. When the economy turned down in the mid-1960s, the embezzlement was painfully apparent. The business failed and my parents lost everything, including our new four-bedroom, two-bath home. As much as anything, the experience branded a lesson in my mind about the importance of doing business with good people you could trust.

As I entered the real world, I discovered that my taste for variety didn't play as well in grown-up environments like the legal profession with its old-boy networks, and the world of business with its unspoken expectations. I had to learn the new rules and the consequences if I broke them. For a stint, I fell in line as I thought a career-minded adult should; I paid more attention to protocol than better possibilities around me. It seemed necessary, especially when the oil bust of the mid-1980s hit the Southern Plains region where my wife and I lived. Bank closures, home foreclosures, job losses, and, sadly, even suicides were the weekly news. The notion of being open-minded felt a bit irrelevant. And yet, while I was grateful to remain employed throughout this season, I couldn't numb the childhood sense of possibility still inside me.

Sometime in my mid-twenties I realized that the gravity of adult life pulls you toward focus and specialization. I began to wonder if that was such a good thing. Have you ever wondered that? We spend four years in college classrooms, and sometimes more, on a narrow bet that we will enjoy and thrive within a specific career for the rest of our lives.

What if you're wrong?

What if you get bored after a few months?

Or, what if you simply have other things you'd also like to do?

Consider this about the narrow bet many place on their

pursuit of success: it's based on a mindset that's over a hundred years old. The strategy of fine-tuning your life originally spread in the early 1900s as agricultural jobs declined and Henry Ford's assembly line expanded the number of industrial jobs in America. With factory jobs in high supply and progress on everyone's mind, our country set in motion an education system that prewired individuals to pick an industry and a skill set and get trained for a long-term career. The broadest opportunity came to people who accepted the promise of stability in exchange for a fine-tuned skill. Uniformity, consistency, and efficiency were praised. What most companies sought was progress via the right protocol and the right people to follow it. These circumstances shaped our grandparents' mindsets. They taught our parents and our parents taught us. So today many still assume it's best to focus on one path and continue to improve.

The trouble is, a lot has changed in the last century.

I'll save the conversation about the capricious nature of today's environment for later. Suffice it to say, for now, that focus and the popular notion of fine-tuning might no longer be the best way to be successful. It's certainly not the most interesting or enjoyable way. It's not the path I've taken.

I'm stepping on some toes now. I know mastery is a hot topic. In his 2008 book, *Outliers*, Malcolm Gladwell famously suggests that it takes 10,000 hours of "deliberate practice" for an individual to reach peak performance in a given skill set. According to Gladwell—who cites a 1993 academic paper by psychologist Anders Ericsson—the "10,000-Hour Rule" is what allowed legends like the Beatles and Bill Gates to achieve such great success.

As the stories go, the young Beatles were plucking guitars in diapers and Gates was pecking at a computer keyboard before he could hold a bottle. As a result, they enjoyed preeminence early in their journeys. I'm exaggerating, of course, but the idea is that these icons locked onto a skill set, gave it singular focus for at least 10,000 hours, and found a great deal of success. I have no issue with hard-line focus; it's required, even forced on us, at times. But when I consider it as a primary success strategy, especially for something like 10,000 hours, three things come to mind.

First, that's a helluva lot of time. To put 10,000 hours in perspective, if you spent three focused hours a day on deliberate practice of a certain skill, it'd take you roughly a decade to get really good. That's not bad if you start in fifth grade but it's an eternity if you're already well into your career. It sounds like a death sentence if you're over fifty.

Second, that sounds incredibly monotonous. While most can appreciate the artistry and precision of an elite performance, few consider the sacrifices necessary for the performer to get there. Winning an Olympic gold medal at eighteen is significant. Forgoing your entire childhood to get there is just as significant, if not more, according to psychologists. A high percentage of Olympic athletes fall into depression after their run for the gold. "It's amazing how many athletes struggle somewhere after the Games," Steven Portenga, the former director of performance psychology for USA Track & Field, told CNN's Ashley Strickland, "because they realize that being an Olympian or having a medal doesn't change their lives typically in a very significant way." There's also the issue of what these athletes, and others who've pursued mastery at all costs, have left behind them. In other words, what leads to their depression is not just falling short of the top medal stand. It's also the cost of trying. Only the individual knows the extent of the sacrifices made, but it's an uneasy thought at the very least when you consider spending half your life or more to achieve something that doesn't quite pan out. Do you really *have* to grind down the same path for many years, sacrificing priorities along the way, in order to be very successful? It's a critical question you should be asking today.

That brings me to my third thought: Is mastery even necessary? Must you become an expert in order to be happy and successful? It certainly hasn't been my experience. In truth, it hasn't been most people's experience. The successful know more than the average person about a particular topic, and/or they possess a better-than-average ability with a particular skill set; but to call them all experts is an enormous stretch. Obviously, in very stable environments like chess or classical music, expertise is necessary if you want to, say, become a grand master or play in the New York Philharmonic one day. However, the vast majority of us work in very unstable environments. Expertise one week can be irrelevant the next. If there's a need for expertise right now, it is—quite paradoxically—in the areas of agility, innovation, and future trends.

"Jack of all trades, master of none" was first penned by a highbrow sixteenth-century author to describe an uneducated, inexperienced playwright he thought naive and unworthy of the trade. It was meant to convey that anyone serious about being a big success must pay his dues and cannot dabble here and there like this particular playwright had been known to do. And this is a common refrain, isn't it? This idea that your level of success must be commensurate to the amount of experience you have in any given field. Your rewards cannot possibly rise above your level of expertise, or so they say. But the story behind "jack of all trades, master of none" is actually amusing—and quite telling.

The name of the self-assured author, the one who claimed the other playwright was a jack of all trades, master of none?

Robert Greene.

You've never heard of him unless you are well versed in the history of British dramatists, which I'm assuming you're probably not.

The playwright whom he described as a "master of none"?

William Shakespeare.

Yes, the same one who wrote *Romeo and Juliet*, *Julius Caesar*, *Othello*, and the list goes on.

The figure of speech that Greene used to describe Shakespeare so long ago is used today to discourage dabbling and encourage a quest for focus and mastery. Yet, the story behind the phrase reveals a completely different moral. What if taking a narrow path is overrated, unsafe, and, frankly, a boring way to do life? And what if specializing isn't the true path to success?

I believe being a master of none offers greater advantages today, in personal and corporate pursuits. The way of variety, of shared leadership, of instability and innovation, clearly paves a path to success, and a life-giving one at that. I hope at the very least that my stories and the lessons they illustrate in the coming pages can convince you that your path to greater success and fulfillment in your career need not follow conventional wisdom.

Here's my point: I'm sure it's gratifying to be the best or even considered among the best at something. But focusing too narrowly comes with its own risks—perhaps even more in today's technology-driven environment, which constantly changes the nature of work and the skills required to do it. Overinvesting in expertise is often riskier than learning to be adaptive and in an always-learning mode. I'll admit up front that if your idea of success is on the level of a mad scientist, holed up in a dim room, working twenty hours a day, eating when you can remember, and showering once a week, then, clearly, mastery is your path. For most people, however, mastery, and its 10,000-hour vision of preeminence, has been largely overrated and overpromised. Studies have already proven this. One in particular was conducted by Princeton University. *Business Insider* reported its findings: "In a meta-analysis of 88 studies on deliberate practice, the researchers found that practice accounted for just a 12 percent difference in performance in various domains." This includes a mere 1 percent difference in professions.

Further, the recent work of top behavioral economists like Daniel Kahneman and Richard Thaler—both Nobel Prize winners—reveals that industry experts with countless hours invested in their craft are prone to overconfidence, making them no better than amateurs at forecasting, say, the housing market's next trend or whether a college football player is worthy of being picked in the first round of the NFL draft.

Findings like these compelled Frans Johansson to write *The Click Moment*, in which he asserts: "There is no doubt that deliberate practice is important, from both a statistical and a theoretical perspective. It is just less important than has been argued." In other words, the value of expertise is often oversold. I believe most of us don't need it to achieve the life we desire.

I don't know about you, but I've chosen to go through life experiencing as much as I can and becoming *good enough* to be successful in a variety of endeavors. That phrase "good enough" might not sit well with you, but when you evaluate the actual benefits of exactitude, you might find, as I have, that becoming good enough to be broadly successful is a better and far more rewarding experience.

I have no desire to be a one-trick pony. It seems rather dull to me. The awards and recognitions that come with a focused career and lifestyle, while meaningful to some degree, don't get me up in the morning. While there's no doubt that devotion can move us closer to success in one arena, one has to consider the real cost to life on the whole and determine how much devotion is really worthwhile and necessary. Will a few hours a week or a few days a month spent chasing other interests really spell the difference between your success and failure? I suppose that depends on what sort of life you're after. Sometimes our truest definition of success requires less focus and sacrifice than we imagine, not more.

In my experience, what matters most in the long run is to succeed on multiple fronts—broadly—enjoying as many days of the week as possible. That can be accomplished by creating a habit of embracing variety in your life and becoming more versatile—by trying more things out. If you do, you won't necessarily become a master of anything, but you don't need to be to usher more life into everything. Instead, you will learn more frequently, expand your horizons more regularly, and have a lot more fun while doing it. In short, you'll start really living.

Yes, I'm the former longtime CEO of a popular public brand called Sonic Drive-In. But it's just a title with which I'm associated, and an incomplete description. I'm really an unfailingly curious boy raised on the Plains who journeyed from middle school scrapper to high school peacekeeper to amateur historian to reluctant attorney with no executive experience who was offered an opportunity to lead in an unfamiliar industry. While I'm grateful to have been in the position of CEO for more than two decades, I've always had many other interests as a lifelong musician who is fascinated by world history, passionate about public education, and always drawn to the adventure of visiting new cities and countries. Don't you have other interests too? Despite my title—or rather, because of my title—I have continued to satisfy my curiosities and chase any new ones that catch my eye. I hope that at some point while reading the pages to come, you decide to do the same. I can't convince you to make one pursuit more important than another. But I will aim to help you see that being more successful and happier in this life doesn't require focusing on one skill set with an eye toward one destination.

I can't write your perfect script for success. Nobody can. But I can tell you that there are more opportunities for success and happiness available to those who are willing to loosen the reins and let themselves wander down many paths. Variety isn't just the spice of life; it's an untapped strategy for succeeding sooner and in more ways than one.

I hope I can free you up to see the real value in being a master of none.

CHAPTER 1

Change Is a Constant

At the heart of it, expertise seems to offer stability. And who doesn't want that? If I can just become a surgeon proficient in one kind of surgery, I will be in high demand, and my life will remain stable. Or if I can practice a very specific kind of business law, then anyone who needs help in that area will come to me, and this expertise will lead to stability. Experts are always in high demand, or at least that's how it looks to us outsiders, and we crave the stability they seem to have.

And it's not just financial stability—it's relational and emotional and mental. As humans, our most ancient ancestors sought security because security meant survival—a stable food source, a stable water supply, and a stable climate meant we could live longer. That instinctual desire for stability and security still motivates a lot of things we do.

But what if I told you stability of any kind is a myth? That seeking it is a waste of time?

That's a lesson I learned early in life, growing up during the tumultuous sixties. By August of 1969, the entire world seemed to be in total chaos. I don't know if people today can understand the hell that was going on back then, or how unsettling it was for a teenage kid. Sixteen months before, Martin Luther King Jr. had been assassinated outside his second-floor room at the Lorraine Motel in Memphis. Two months later, Robert Kennedy was mortally wounded in the Ambassador Hotel in Los Angeles. And both came just a few years removed from the November 1963 assassination of President John F. Kennedy. During the 1960s, it seemed like anything could happen at any time. There were marches taking place all around the country aimed at racial equality, and the United States was entrenched in Vietnam, a confusing conflict that seemed like it might never end.

In the eye of all of that historical chaos, my twin sister and I started our freshman year at Northwest Classen High School in Oklahoma City, having moved there in 1966 after our dad lost his business and our family lost our home. This might sound a bit anticlimactic compared with the events swirling around us, but it would be unlike any year of school we had started before, because 1969 was the year that Oklahoma City began desegregating our public-school system. Court cases regarding the desegregation of high schools and universities had been going on for literally decades leading up to the sixties, and the initial *Brown v. Board of Education* had been argued in front of the United States Supreme

Court in the fifties, but it turned out that actually integrating the schools was a completely different matter. States dragged their feet. School districts looked for work-arounds to avoid it, some concerned with the effects publicity would have on the students, some worried about potential outbreaks of violence, and others simply acting on racist convictions. It eventually took a further ruling by the Supreme Court, that "fear of social unrest or violence, whether real or constructed by those wishing to oppose integration, does not excuse state governments from complying with *Brown*."[1] Schools in our country had no final excuse. They had to integrate black and white students.

So, there we were, my sister and I, thrust into the middle of a high school actively being desegregated. It was wild, and the prevailing attitude in our community was that desegregation would prove to be a mistake. The federal judge who had ordered the desegregation of Oklahoma City Public Schools had a likeness of him burned in effigy, hanging from a bridge over one of the busier streets in the city. My family, and especially my parents, were vocal supporters of desegregation, and when I heard about that burning in effigy, I hoped my family would be safe.

One of the major players in everything going on in Oklahoma City at the time was a woman named Clara Luper. Luper had attended segregated schools but was the first African American to enroll in the University of Oklahoma's history department, obtaining her master's degree in 1951. But she didn't stop there—she became one of the foundational leaders of the civil rights movement in our state, facilitating some of the earliest sit-ins in Oklahoma. It was their main method of protest, and, through the efforts of people like Luper, African Americans were able to push for integration of all kinds of public facilities in Oklahoma by the mid-sixties: restaurants and bathrooms and buses.[2] She fought hard to integrate the Oklahoma schools as well.

In those first weeks of high school, the situation was tense, and grew more challenging thereafter. Eventually there were police and U.S. marshals everywhere: in the parking lot, outside the entrance, and in the hallways. Dark-skinned and light-skinned kids eyed the officers and one another suspiciously. A few weeks into the semester, I learned that one of the history teachers in our high school was Miss Clara Mae Luper, the civil rights icon. I had no idea I was living in a history book. Few of us do come to this realization until well after the fact.

What a time. This was the context in which I started high school, but it wasn't only the public-school system that was experiencing wrenching growing pains. Even my parents had gone through big changes in the sixties, particularly in how they viewed individual rights and freedom. Their changing views placed us squarely in the crosshairs of an often unkind, aggressively racist culture. My mom and dad went from being Republicans all their lives to supporting Hubert Humphrey for president in 1968, and even registering as Democrats. They felt that strongly about civil rights.

My mother was a teacher in an Oklahoma City school,

having gone back to school herself to get her college degree after my father's business had failed several years before all this. And she didn't choose to go teach in a privileged, suburban school—she was a white teacher in a segregated, all-black elementary school on the east side of town. She was sensitive to what my sister and I were experiencing during the desegregation of our high school, and both she and my father were determined to remain vocally supportive of the efforts.

Watching how my parents conducted themselves during those years taught me a lot about patience and perseverance, diplomacy and shrewdness, and how important it is to ally yourself with the right people. In fact, they were the ones who first taught me to stand for what I thought was important, no matter what the consequences might be. It was probably at that age when I began to realize that the world would always be in flux, and my best bet wasn't to throw down an anchor to try to stabilize my boat but to figure out the best way to ride out the waves. When you realize that nothing is going to stay the same, you can begin adjusting for the potential changes that might come your way.

• • •

THE FOUR YEARS I spent at Northwest Classen High School were enormously formative, for that stage of life and for the rest of my life. The school was a good one. Each year it produced several National Merit finalists, and its graduates include Senator Elizabeth Warren, a 2020 Democratic presidential candidate; Ed Ruscha, the pop artist known for his 1966 piece "Standard Station" and many other great works; Mason Williams, the composer and comedian perhaps best known for his 1968 instrumental hit "Classical Gas" and his work on *The Smothers Brothers Comedy Hour*; Vince Gill, the country-music artist who has earned twenty-one Grammys and eighteen CMA Awards in his career; and me! The unique experiences, the values developed, the friendships made, and my growth as a young leader there would set me on a different course and serve me well for a lifetime.

My family had just moved to the area before my freshman year, so I didn't begin the year with strong friendships or a sense of where I fit into the school's social scene, notwithstanding the racial and political tensions that were brewing in the larger community.

One day in my freshman history class, we were receiving routine instructions from Larry Mott and Ophelia Byers, our team teachers who were really exceptional. (Even now, fifty years later, I use an outlining method taught to me by them whenever I prepare a presentation.)

In the hallway outside the classroom an ugly fight broke out between a group of students. Several male students in the class moved to the door, only to be confronted by Miss Byers, who put her entire sixty-five-plus-year-old frame across the door and said, "You're not going anywhere! Sit down!" It was a good thing too, because the horrible fight outside our classroom resulted in one student being stabbed in the chest. He was rushed to the hospital and survived, but the repercussions from the day stayed with us: we weren't safe and secure, not even in the halls of our high school. While my senses were on alert, I was not one of the students who had rushed to the door that day. I was learning to be prepared for everything but also not to dive in when emotions run high.

I can't say the same for many of the parents after that day, particularly the white parents. Their behavior before that incident had been poor, but they now went into a rage. No longer were there merely phone calls to the administration and requested meetings; parents now began showing up on campus in groups demanding to speak to someone in charge. For months, there was hardly a week that went by without hearing raised adult voices from the school office or parking lot, and occasionally even the classrooms. It would be years before I would see adults behave so badly again. The experience was so unsettling and in such contrast to how I witnessed my parents behaving that a desire began stirring inside me.

Toward the end of my freshman year, I attended an all-student assembly at which four candidates were standing for president of the student council for the next year. I was mesmerized by the prospect of one student, any student, not only receiving the vote of confidence from his or her peers through an election but also winning the responsibility to steward their trust and make good decisions for every student at the school. It was at that moment, sitting in that student assembly, that I decided I would be standing on the stage of a future assembly.

I immediately laid plans to run for student council my sophomore year and did run for sophomore class vice president. Why vice president? Because five or six people filed for president—and no one filed for vice president. I won without a challenge.

In approaching my junior year, I observed that each of the prior junior class presidents had run for student council president later and had lost. The burden of raising money to sponsor the junior/senior prom seemed to leave the junior class president with a credibility deficit. I made the decision to avoid incurring that same deficit altogether.

Instead, I was encouraged to pursue the presidency of the Human Relations Club, a group of students who worked toward reducing racial tension and increasing diversity engagement and understanding. This seemed like a good cause and a good way to expand my set of friends. Both were accurate—and accompanied by a very public process of engaging with KOSO (Keep Our Schools Open), a student-led, citywide effort to ensure our school bond vote passed in spite of the anti-integration effort of some patrons to undermine the public-school system. (The bond vote did pass, with active KOSO telephone banks, press conferences, mailings, and the like.)

At the end of my junior year, I took my place in that

same student assembly, appealing to my classmates to become student council president as one of four candidates, including two white students and two black students (ironically, each named White). On the first ballot, I received 56 percent of the vote, winning without a runoff.

And so, in my senior year, I had my first significant experience in leadership and team building, setting goals, ensuring diverse participation, and moving the collection of students through a series of activities throughout the school year. My fellow elected officers and the collective group included both young men and women of diverse backgrounds and ethnicity. (Our treasurer, an African American girl, today assists me with asset management in her professional capacity.) One of the more unique experiences included bringing together the student council presidents from all of the city's public high schools with a public appeal to parents to let students iron out difficulties in their schools, without parental interference. The press conference hit the front page of the newspaper the next day.

I completed high school a markedly different person than I began—more mature and with the realization that it was important to bring people with different opinions and backgrounds together, not only to solve problems that plagued everyone but also to make positive progress. These leadership skills set me on a path I've come to understand and appreciate only with the passage of time.

• • •

MY MOM WASN'T the only one in the family deeply involved in education and the community. When an opportunity presented itself to my dad, he jumped right in too.

During the previous decade, a judge by the name of Luther Bohanon had handled the controversial school desegregation case *Dowell v. Board of Education of Oklahoma City Public Schools*. Bohanon found, against popular opinion, that the Oklahoma City Public School District was operating a dual education system—east side schools filled with poor and racial minorities, west side schools filled with whites, and the northwest quadrant filled with well-equipped schools—something that violated the Equal Protection Clause of the Fourteenth Amendment to the U.S. Constitution. And a few years after I started high school, Bohanon would also be the one to order the district to create a plan that would bus children from various areas of our school districts into other areas, basically the final move of desegregating the Oklahoma City Public School system.[3]

As you can imagine, this didn't go over well in the community. Years later, I became good friends with the judge's son, Richard Bohanon, who was also a federal judge. Richard described the scarring effect the events of the late sixties and early seventies had had on his father. After ordering desegregation of the school district, Judge Bohanon, according to his son, had difficulty attending his own church—so hot were emotions after his decision.

Around the time I started high school, District Judge Bohanon and his magistrate had formed a sounding board called the Biracial Committee, a group of concerned citizens who could provide a grassroots view of the impact desegregation was having, how it was affecting the city, and ideas on how to keep moving it forward. This, by the way, is the definition of diversifying your expectations and planning on the inevitability of instability. It rests on the belief that expertise is widely distributed among a collective group—not held in the hands of one person. The judge could have pushed his own plan through, fighting anything and anyone who came up against his preconceived ideas on how things would go, come hell or high water. But the judge and magistrate didn't. They put together this panel to stay ahead of the curve and prepare themselves to deal with the instability of the times, with the hope that, if given the chance, individual members of the community would come forth with ideas worthy of consideration and implementation.

The judge asked for volunteers in the community, people who would be willing to serve on the panel. I can't remember how long the term was, but it was a big commitment, both because of the time involved and because of the spotlight placed on the issue in those days. Those who supported maintaining a segregated school district saw those on the panel as die-hard supporters of desegregation; in other words, their archenemies. Despite all of that, the judge got a good number of people who were willing to volunteer. My dad was one of them, and I think he was one of the few white men in the private business sector willing to serve on such a panel—there was plenty of motivation for businessmen to avoid that kind of controversy—so not only did the judge select him, he even appointed my dad to serve as the chairman.

My parents certainly weren't pursuing or embracing stability. If they had been, they would have moved out of the city's public-school district or put me in a private school (not that they could have easily afforded that). Or they could have encouraged all of us in the family to keep our heads down and get through those years as smoothly as possible. But they didn't do that. They put themselves in the crosshairs, leading with their beliefs and prepared for the instability to come.

When my siblings and I returned from school every day, the discussion was not about sports or trivial matters. Most nights, around the dinner table, the conversation was about politics, the events my mother was witnessing firsthand in her segregated school, or the hot topics my dad was wading through on the Biracial Committee. There were so many angles to what was going on. As the months passed, things didn't get any easier—our city's struggle with desegregation and racism continued to cause problems.

My freshman year, Northwest Classen had a basketball game with a long-standing rival, a segregated inner-city school with 100 percent African American kids. The game was at their high school, so four of my friends and I headed over that night to watch. Our desegregated high school basketball team made the mistake of winning the game. Afterward, a brawl broke out in the parking lot involving perhaps a dozen students from both schools.

The five of us got separated out there, hiding behind cars,

trying to avoid the fights that were breaking out around us. Later, I would find out that two of my friends got roughed up, and one got stabbed in the back. He was loaded up in someone else's car and driven to the hospital. But I didn't know that at the time. I was just trying to get out of there.

I was sneaking toward the VW we had come in, and when I finally got to it, the driver was in the car. He unlocked it, motioned for me to hurry up, and I hopped in. He looked pretty startled, and of the five of us, I was the only one who emerged unscathed. Our other friends finally joined us, and we heard that the last member of our group had been taken to the hospital.

We drove off. There was upheaval all around us in those days, which had a profound effect on my personality and my worldview. Those years conditioned me for a life of continuous evolution and change.

• • •

TO BE HONEST, though, I thrived in this kind of an environment. I'm not completely sure why—maybe it's because I was the little brother among four kids, all of us very close in age, and if I wanted something, I had to really go for it. Or maybe it was because my parents' expansive interests gave me eclectic tastes—they loved education, music, and politics, and they talked about those things with us all the time. They had a huge influence on me.

Another possible reason for my adventurous nature and

ability to thrive in chaos is that I have a very short attention span. The stimulation of new topics is always welcome. I also had the opportunity to watch the way my parents engaged with people from all walks of life, treating them with respect and curiosity, and I learned the value and joy of connecting with the world in this same manner.

My family's social attitudes had consequences, as all important ones do. My dad experienced social pressure and was ostracized for his views. There were a lot of people in Oklahoma City who thought we should fight harder for segregation, fight longer to keep children separated by race. They thought bringing white and black children together to learn would be the end of things as we knew them. My dad's views threatened them in some way, hitting on their fears or concerns or prejudices, and they didn't like it.

When I ran for student body president my senior year, the president of the PTA told her son to tell kids in our school not to vote for me because if I was elected, I would only do things that would further desegregate our schools. Sure, it was true that I was supportive of desegregation, but I still thought that it was interesting the PTA president was concerned about working with me because of my family's views.

It didn't stop at the president of the PTA. Even the principal of the high school had similar concerns about my family, about me. At a point when there were four of us running for the position of president, he quietly went to one of the other nominees, the young man he considered to be my biggest competitor, and coached him on the best strategy to use in spending his campaign money, hoping to increase the likelihood that I would lose. The principal knew that I had already spent all the money I was allowed to spend for the duration of the campaigning period, so he told the other kid to hold on to some money in case he ended up in a runoff with me—then he'd have money left to spend.

Much later, after I'd won the position and thrived for a time, the principal told me he had been concerned about my election, that I might be a rabble-rouser, but he was pleased, in the end, with how I had worked with everyone from all sides. He was impressed with my negotiating skills and transparency. These were skills I had seen my parents exhibiting, and operating in that position gave me the chance to practice what they had taught me.

Finding my way through periods of instability is an important skill to learn at such an early age. It's all the more important to deploy when you're an adult.

• • •

I THINK ABOUT my father navigating his way through the Biracial Committee he chaired. I think about my mother advocating on behalf of her inner-city students. I think of Judge Bohanon persevering through the minefield that was the 1960s. What did they all have in common? Conviction.

The people who've had the greatest influence on my life—and, arguably, the world—were those who believed in something so passionately that it gave them roots. Roots that went deep underground, keeping them upright and nourished. Those people taught me that in an inevitably unstable world, the best hope we have is a strong foundation, one that's the sum total of our intuition, intelligence, belief, courage, determination, and self-expectations.

When I think of historical figures known for their tremendous conviction, one person comes to mind: Nelson Mandela. As the leader of the African National Congress, Mandela led the charge against the pro-apartheid government, which institutionalized the separation of races. In 1964, he was sentenced to life in prison for sabotage and plotting revolution. During his twenty-seven-year imprisonment, he spent the first eighteen at a former leper colony off the coast of Cape Town, where he was confined to a small cell without a bed or plumbing and was required to do hard labor in a lime quarry. He was only allowed visits from his wife and two young daughters once every six months, and he endured inhumane punishments, such as guards burying inmates in the ground up to their necks and urinating on them.

During that time, the South African government was getting pressured by Mandela's followers, and the authorities thought that if they could release him on their terms, it might be better for them if he was no longer in prison. They went on to offer him at least three conditional offers of release, and he refused each one.

"I cannot and will not give any undertaking at a time when I and you, the people, are not free," his daughter read in a statement from Mandela. "Your freedom and mine cannot be separated." What is the point of accepting the government offer, he said, when apartheid still effectively reduces freedom to almost nothing? His statement ended with: "I cherish my own freedom dearly, but I care even more for your freedom."

What a genius response. Conviction at its finest.

In 1990, South Africa had a newly elected president—F. W. de Klerk—who ordered Mandela's release. For the next three years, Mandela led negotiations for an end to apartheid and the establishment of a multiracial government. In 1994, with his people finally free, he became the first president of South Africa to be elected in a fully representative democratic election.

The ability to negotiate played no small role in Mandela securing peace and transitioning South Africa out of apartheid. The man started negotiating while he was in prison, for goodness' sake! He had almost zero leverage, at least to the untrained eye, yet he was able to end apartheid and improve the living conditions of black South Africans. There are certainly lessons to be learned from what he was able to accomplish, one of which is, you don't have to be best friends with those on the other side of the negotiating table, but you do have to keep the lines of communication open.

Mr. Mandela argued with Mr. de Klerk constantly, often disagreeing about the cause of the violence that plagued their country. After one particularly heated exchange, Mr. de Klerk hung up, slamming the phone down. But somehow Mr. Mandela ensured that contact between the two sides continued.

"We would both frequently have to rise above our personal antipathy," Mr. de Klerk once said while reflecting on those years of communication between him and Mandela.

I think about many years later, visiting Mandela's destination cell in Johannesburg, the jailhouse converted to a courthouse, Robben Island, and his home. The changes he stood for, years in the making, brought about by his conviction. I think about many years before, the many conversations my dad had with other white businessmen with whom he vehemently disagreed, trying to maintain a relationship in order to keep those lines of communication open. I think of my small example serving as high school student council president at a newly integrated high school, appearing on the front page of a local newspaper with fellow high school student council presidents—male and female, black and white—suggesting our parents back off and let their kids come together and work things out.

To stand firm doesn't mean unmoving. But standing firm in an unstable environment . . . if I learned anything from those late teen years of my life, I certainly learned the benefit of that.

RULE OF THUMB #1:
Stability Is a Myth.

Time and again, the people and circumstances in my life taught me that either we stand on convictions or we stand on nothing. But the simultaneous, perhaps conflicting, idea here is that we should be prepared for change by remaining open, flexible, and nimble; that in order to handle life's ever-present shifts, we must be willing to bend. How can we do both? Is it possible to stand firm and surrender at the same time?

I liken it to stretching every day for the purpose of remaining flexible. The benefits of stretching our muscles are many: improved elasticity, increased range of motion, and injury prevention, just to name a few. Ask any physician or physical therapist and they'll agree on its importance, whether they're advocating for daily, weekly, static, active, or ballistic stretching. They'll also agree that consistent stretching does us no good if we're not also fueling our muscles through regular activity.

Have you ever had an injury that required rehabilitation? A critical facet of the treatment plan is stretching; it's the crux that dramatically speeds up the recovery process by permanently reorganizing the scar fibers and allowing the circulation to become normal. If you have an injured leg, a couple weeks into rehab will reveal pliable leg muscles as a result of stretching, which in turn will have promoted gentle healing. But flexibility will have only taken you so far because, regardless, your leg muscles will have shrunk; despite the positive effects of stretching, atrophy is the inevitable reaction to underuse.

If we claim to be open and flexible, yet all we do is sit in the same chair and do the same thing day in and day out, then what is the point of flexibility? Remaining nimble as a way to prepare for change does us no good if, when the change comes, our muscles have atrophied. We can all say we're open to change and to new opportunities, but the reality is if we don't practice changing—if we don't activate our muscles, so to speak—we're not going to be able to use that so-called flexibility when we actually have to change.

Life

No matter where you find yourself in life—married, single, kids, pets, employed, retired—you surely know that for everything there is a season. Nothing is forever, or even consistent; priorities shift, people grow, and dreams evolve. In response to those continuous changes, those fundamental instabilities, there's often a tendency to self-preserve. Protecting ourselves against the unknown by keeping our guard up is the reason humans have built walls to keep others out, or in, for at least the last 12,000 years. Is your theoretical wall protecting you, but in doing so, keeping others out?

In life, the way you remain flexible and alive is by, ironically, fighting against the urge for self-preservation. So often we resist change and flexibility in the name of preserving ourselves for our jobs, our main work, the things that "really matter." How many times have you put something off because you have to get up early for work the next morning?

How many times have you avoided a conversation or not entertained a thought due to a pressing matter that's taking up a lot of brain space? How many times have you admitted to yourself that those are just excuses? Think about all the positive that could come out of resisting the urge to use self-preservation to the detriment of flexibility.

Work

The World Economic Forum's *Future of Jobs Report 2018* estimates that by 2022, roughly 75 million jobs will be displaced due to a shift in the division of labor between humans and machines. We live in a tumultuous time because of technology, and it puts us in a dog-eat-dog world, no matter what job you have. It's no wonder we want to lay claim to the ideas that are ours and make sure everybody knows they're ours. We don't want to be overlooked, miss our opportunity for promotion, or lose our jobs—to robots or otherwise. We get defensive and hold tightly to what we feel we've justifiably earned. Whether we're cognizant of it or not, that defensiveness is what closes us off and can become our undoing.

We can't learn or become better at our jobs if we hold tightly to an inflexible and overprotective mindset. We can't flourish in our roles if we succumb to the tendency of not helping others or being unwilling to receive help from others—we won't learn anything new or become better at our jobs that way, since, often in our jobs, we become better from the people around us. We learn from the people who've gone before us, but also from new people who come in afterward and offer a new perspective. Cutting ourselves off from those people and all they offer only means we're hindering our own growth.

Leadership

As a leader, how do you keep your muscles activated? How do you keep them from atrophying? One of the easiest, and likely underutilized, ways to remain both flexible and strong within your leadership position is through accessibility and listening. That is, being available for conversations and then being actively present while having them.

Many leaders say they're accessible, but when it comes down to it, they're too busy, too distracted, too ill at ease, or too egocentric to make themselves readily available. Where do you fall? Maybe you place productivity ahead of approachability, or maybe you lend yourself to others through alternatives like comment or idea boxes. If that's the case, as a leader, do you actually read those entries? Or do you off-load that task to a staff member or intern and instruct them to tell you which ones they think are important?

Anybody can pay lip service, but only a leader with integrity can make the time to meet with and actively listen to those under his or her leadership. The days of the leader in the ivory tower are long gone, or at least they should be. True accessibility can only be achieved through more face-to-face communication, more conversations, and listening to more voices.

CHAPTER 2

Control Is an Illusion

In 1997, my second complete fiscal year as CEO, with Sonic forty-four years old, our brand hit $1 billion in systemwide sales for the first time. In only four more years, Sonic doubled to $2 billion in systemwide sales. How did I muscle this through? I didn't.

More on that later.

• • •

GENERAL GEORGE PATTON wanted to be a war hero from a very young age, having grown up listening to stories of his ancestors' involvement in the American Revolution and the Civil War. I can just picture him sitting with his father or grandfather beside the fire or around the dinner table, his eyes wide, absorbing their stories. Once he was old enough, he attended the U.S. Military Academy at West Point (as everyone expected him to), proved himself to be a talented swordsman, and even competed in the Olympic Pentathlon in Stockholm in 1912. Everything he did as a young man was focused on one thing: learning as much as he could about the strategies of war.

He made a splash in WWI, operating as the first officer assigned to the new American Expeditionary Force tank corps. And he was hugely successful in that role, quickly moving up the ranks in the coming years.

"We shall attack and attack until we are exhausted, and then we shall attack again." General Patton's seemingly unquenchable desire for battle earned him the moniker "Old Blood and Guts" from his soldiers. He was an unflinching man. His harsh and unrelenting discipline, aggressive approach, and complete lack of fear allowed the United States to recover from a series of losses and regain momentum against the Nazis by winning the Battle of El Guettar in March of 1943.

But a month later, General Patton would come under criticism after he struck a soldier suffering from shell shock, calling him a coward. He would eventually issue a public apology.[4] But it doesn't seem like anyone was surprised by this abrasive interaction: This was his leadership style. This was who he was.

He later led the U.S. forces over the Rhine River, capturing 10,000 miles of territory and playing a key role in the liberation of Germany from Nazi rule. Soon, the general came under fire again when he became a vocal critic of the Allies' denazification policies in Germany. He was removed from his position as commander of the Third Army in October of 1945. Only a few months later, in December, he broke his neck in an automobile accident, dying twelve days later in Heidelberg.

General Patton's leadership style worked in the environment of war—his autocratic, "my way or the highway" manner was effective in moving men across battlefields, motivating them to get up out of the trenches and charge. And maybe his style was exactly what was needed at that point. But the field of battle was where his leadership experience began and ended. I have to wonder, if General Patton had survived beyond World War II, what would his life have been like? I don't think his approach would have worked outside of the military in the fifties and sixties.

Would he have ever left the corridors of war? I doubt it. Why? Because he believed in maintaining rigid control of everyone under his rank. In just about every area of life outside of the military, complete control is a complete illusion. If I would wake up in the morning and go into the office with a General Patton attitude, demanding 100 percent obedience, expecting to control everyone around me as if they were robots, my team would quickly become disoriented, disillusioned, and disinterested. You cannot foster a dynamic team through strict control.

Could there have been a leader more different from General Patton than General Dwight D. Eisenhower?

Within seven years of the end of World War II, in 1952,

Eisenhower announced he would be running for the Republican presidential nomination. He had never served in an elected office before that.

On November 4, 1952, Eisenhower was elected president of the United States in a landslide victory. So what was it about Eisenhower that allowed him to make a successful transition from the rigid leadership structure in the military to the political world where things like consensus and compromise are required? How could two men raised in similar eras and who excelled through the same rigorous training from childhood end up with such different approaches?

Many people have heard of the plaque on Harry Truman's desk that read "The buck stops here." Well, Eisenhower also had a desk decoration that made a statement: his was a paperweight placed in a prominent position, but on it was a Latin inscription that translated to "gently in manner, strong in deed." This epitomized his leadership style. He wasn't the kind of person to rule with an iron fist the way Patton did. He didn't puff out his chest and steamroll people. He did everything in his power to bring people along with him.

"Together we must learn to compose differences, not with arms, but with intellect and decent purpose," Eisenhower once said.

But he didn't bring just anyone along with him, and he didn't only bring along people who agreed with him. He surrounded himself with people who fit one criterion: they were lifelong learners willing not only to share what they'd learned with others but to learn from others too. Eisenhower leaned heavily on the counsel of such people as, I imagine, they did his. "Always try to associate yourself with, and learn as much as you can from, those who know more than you do, who do better than you, who see more clearly than you."

• • •

IF THERE'S ONE thing I've learned in my years of leadership, it's the crucial importance of surrounding yourself with people who can educate you on topics in which you're deficient. No leader knows everything, even if he or she acts like it. In fact, if a leader acts all-knowing, it's a sure sign he's not. I've always intended to get my own paperweight that had the inscription: "If you're the smartest person in the room, you're in the wrong room." It's a belief in this kind of interdependence that had a huge impact on the way I ran Sonic.

There would be plenty of jobs that reported to the CEO (me) for which I had very little basic knowledge. I decided that deference to others, and the knowledge they had gained over the years, would be critical in moving the company forward. Based on my position, sure, I could boss people around and make their lives miserable, but I knew that neither of those would contribute to the kind of company I wanted to be involved in. Nor would it be a productive use of time, which I knew was going to suddenly become less available.

A lot of CEOs are agenda-related and fearful of the unknown, of surprises. A lot of organizations spend a lot of resources protecting the CEO, making sure the CEO isn't surprised or doesn't hear what they don't want to hear. What if I did the opposite? What if I allowed things to occur rather than attempting to control them? What if I led with an openness, a willingness to let others in the organization engage and follow through? What if I stood back and allowed those processes to occur? Not only would it be convenient—because at the beginning of my tenure as a CEO I really didn't know what I didn't know—but in the long run, did I really want to micromanage people who were perfectly qualified to manage themselves? That's not to say I wouldn't bend over backward to get familiar with all the different facets of the company. I worked incredibly hard at handling the duties of the CEO, trying to exceed the expectations of my position. But even on that first day, when my predecessor abruptly left the building, I knew I'd have a better chance if I trusted the team of people around me.

• • •

GROWING UP, MY sport of choice was baseball. I thrived in that environment, found myself inherently respecting and valuing the interconnectedness of the team members. I usually batted second or third in the order and could appreciate the coach's strategy of placing us according to our natural strengths. The leadoff hitter was the guy who could be trusted to hit the ball and get on base; he was also usually the fastest kid, because if he got on first base, he could probably steal. The second in the lineup needed to have good contact and enough speed to mirror the leadoff batter. The third at-bat didn't need to be a homerun hitter; he just needed to put the ball in motion in order to advance the previous runners. The fourth was the cleanup spot, the power hitter who could bring everyone home. We all understood that everyone in the lineup was integral to the team, and everyone's skill set served a unique purpose.

Lessons like that were ingrained in me from a young age and continued to develop during my time in student government. Even though I was the one representing the student body, I had a team of other students surrounding me who did their jobs so I could do mine. I also progressively absorbed leadership lessons because of my lifetime enjoyment of reading historical biographies. Isn't it wonderful that in our hands we can hold the successes and failures of those who came before us? When it came to leadership, as well as a great many other things, they made mistakes so we wouldn't have to.

By reading about leaders like General Patton, I learned that steamrolling people never really works—and especially not in a franchised organization like Sonic, where every restaurant represents a corporate entity entrusting an individual entrepreneur with the tools and support to expand a successful brand. I was given the job of leading hundreds of independent franchisees, each helmed by strong entrepreneurs in their own right whom I needed to come alongside and encourage. That model alone requires letting go of a ton of control. As the franchisor, we needed to set parameters around acceptable operations, but that's much different from controlling every aspect of the endeavor.

Leaders often make the mistake of putting pressure on themselves to decide alone what any particular outcome needs to be. Then they try to convince others that their outcome is the right one, pushing as hard as they can to execute that outcome. Approaching a problem with this kind of rigid, outcome-based leadership model completely eliminates your ability to learn on the fly, and it doesn't account for the talents and skills of the other members of your team. When you predetermine an outcome and then impose attainment of that outcome on your team, you're asking for problems.

Inspired by leaders like President Eisenhower, I've learned to set an objective at the outset, but instead of making that objective the absolute focus, I spend more of my time figuring out the "who" of the problem—in other words, making sure the right people are involved in what's going on. In his well-known book *Good to Great*, Jim Collins famously called this getting the right people on the bus. If I know I have the right "who" involved, I can let go of the reins in any situation, sit back, and see what happens. This leads to all kinds of wonderful, unexpected outcomes, new lines of thinking, and fresh direction, none of which would ever have occurred if I had provided my team with a hard-line outcome and steps to accomplish it.

Even to this day, all these years later, I have the same attitude as I did when I started as CEO. I had to manage a lot of things about which I don't have expert knowledge. Someone looking in from the outside might think otherwise, but I couldn't possibly know everything I needed to know to run Sonic. This is true for any CEO, any director, and anyone who leads people—we can never know everything there is to know. Whether it's technology or distribution, food specifications or food science, I simply don't have the expertise required. So, what do I do? How can I effectively lead a group of people when I don't have all the answers?

This is the only way to lead people, in my opinion—always remembering that you don't have all the answers. Because luckily, you don't have to.

I rely on people who know more than me on any subject at hand, if not more than one. Any leader who thinks they can know everything, make every decision, and have a good handle on all knowledge is heading for burnout, failure, and a team around them who feels underappreciated and untrusted. Because I know I can't be proficient in everything, I've utilized a process that helps me ask the right questions and build a strategic plan that gets us going in the right direction.

When I say I'm not rigidly focused on one outcome from the beginning, this doesn't mean I am operating without any kind of structure or process. Look, when you're involved in a multibillion-dollar business, having a process is crucial. So, what's mine?

Let's say someone comes to me with a path they'd like

to pursue, either a revision to existing plans or a completely new idea. There are three key things I immediately want to know from them, three things that will play a huge role in determining where we're going to go next. I would ask my staff:

- What is our objective?
- What process will we utilize?
- Who is at the table?

If I'm convinced they are onto something based on their answers to those three questions, then we go to the next appropriate step. Sometimes, we might get buy-in from the management team regarding the outcome and process, but it's only me and my next-door buddy working on the project. Well, we probably don't have the right people at the table, so we either scrap the idea or dig further into who a better "who" might be. If this was the case, we'd have to sit down as a group and review who we could add to the team to help us realize our outcome.

This process, these three questions, they're not rocket science—but they're effective because they remove any preconceived bias I might have about the process or the outcome. It might be hard for me to see the outcome that they see clearly, or maybe I am not sold on the process, but then they introduce me to the team working on it, and it's an all-star group, and suddenly I'm coming around, getting excited about the possibilities, and better understanding the idea and what they're trying to accomplish, all because they've got the right people moving it forward.

This very thing happened in 1995 when we were conducting a systemwide license renegotiation. The thirteen-month process yielded a new agreement that gave us, the franchisor, the authority to require consistent menus, uniforms, facilities, and purchasing contracts that enabled us to become more of a "brand" and less of a confederation.

In my view, the biggest challenge was not getting the new, contractual authority; the biggest challenge was selling it to our independently minded franchisees. It was a tall order that needed to be handled with a perfect mix of delicacy, authority, and innovation. And the only officer of our company whom I thought could readily sell the proposed plan to our franchise leadership was our CMO, Pattye Moore.

Pattye had been with the company only two to three years at that point. She had come to us from our ad agency, whose founder died shortly after she joined us, and the agency folded. She was very bright, very hardworking, and enjoyed her strong relationship with our franchise leadership.

I approached Pattye about assuming the responsibility for this brand-building effort, which we were calling Sonic 2000. She hesitated until she learned another officer opposed her assuming the assignment, and then her competitive juices kicked in. As was the case with most everything she came to work on, though, she was front, center, proficient, and productive.

I confidently handed over the reins to Pattye because my

three questions were answered with significant clarity and transparency. We aligned on the objective: to bring greater consistency and higher quality to our food, employee uniforms, and physical facilities. I knew the process that would be utilized: Pattye would lead a broad array of "Dream Team" meetings with operators at all levels. I knew who was at the table: Pattye at the lead, with our management team and franchise leadership all engaged.

With that, knowing Pattye's attention to detail, utter competency, and credibility, I was comfortable turning loose day-to-day activities. And that delegation was richly rewarded: store-level profits increased almost 50 percent in the late 1990s, new store openings took off, and systemwide sales doubled from $1 billion to $2 billion from 1997 to 2001. She had some help along the way (see chapter 6), but Pattye worked harder and more diligently than she would have had I made any attempt to manage her closely.

Engagement of the team was essential, and delegation of responsibilities all the more so. And my decision to let go gave Pattye the opportunity to significantly grow and develop new skills as a leader, which had a lasting impact on her. And the value and strength of our brand moved to a different place altogether.

• • •

THINK ABOUT THE most tired you've ever been in your life. Despite what you might initially think, it probably wasn't when you stayed the latest at work, or when you came home from a trip after a delayed flight and unexpected layover. It was probably when you had someone looking over your shoulder, watching your every move. Am I right?

In a recent study conducted in the U.K., researchers placed activity trackers on a hundred hospital employees during a twelve-hour shift. At the end of the shift, the employees were asked, "Do you feel fatigued?" The responses were surprising. It wasn't the people who moved the most who felt the most fatigued, but the people who didn't feel they had control over their jobs.[5]

I know relinquishing control isn't everyone's natural tendency. The old adage "If you want something done right, do it yourself" is famous for a reason. As a leader, someone may take their position to mean they can force their will on others (or on an entire organization), try to manage external events, and make things happen their way. Have you worked for someone like that? Then you can relate to the emotional exhaustion, low morale, poor communication, lack of innovation, and risk aversion that ensue.

When I was a young lawyer, one of my superiors held unattainably high standards for those who worked under him. He applied too much pressure as a way to increase productivity. I'll admit that, initially, it often worked and there would be a temporary spike in performance. But over time, as motivation dropped off, so did productivity. If he had relinquished some of his control, he would have empowered his subordinates and colleagues to show more initiative, giving us the self-confidence to *want* to be effective and advantageous.

Paradoxically, it is only by relinquishing control that leaders can ever become great leaders. Control revolves around dominance, directing, measuring performance, and taking corrective action. Leadership, on the other hand, is all about influence. It's based on setting clear objectives, delegating authority, trusting staff, and inspiring others; it's the capacity to have an effect on the character, development, or behavior of someone or something. Notice the use of "an effect" versus "control." To swap those would give leadership an entirely new meaning.

It comes down to this: How you implement your influence, with just the right balance between exerting and relinquishing control, will determine your ongoing, sustainable level of success as a leader. You don't have to control to have impact. You do, however, have to be clear about your objectives, use good processes, and have the right people at the table.

RULE OF THUMB #2:
Your Impact Is Greater When You're Not in Complete Control.

Control is about trust—or the lack thereof. We tend to trust ourselves a great deal more easily than we trust others, but that's a limiting strategy. It's also unsustainable, impractical, and unhealthy. Even if we *could* do everything ourselves, we shouldn't. Not only does it strip other capable people of their confidence, but it puts far more on our plate than is feasible to manage. We need to begin to elevate and invest our trust in others, and the best way to do that is by giving them regular opportunities to increase that trust.

Tony Hsieh, the CEO of the online shoe and clothing company Zappos, is a prime example of what I'm talking about. Of the roughly 1,500 employees Hsieh oversees, 500 of them work at the Zappos call center and field over 7,000 phone calls per day.[6] When talking to customers, the agents don't use scripts and never respond with phrases like "That's against our policy" or "Let me get a supervisor." Instead, they cater solutions to each customer, and are empowered to do so because of the one rule Hsieh has in their company handbook: Be yourself and use your best judgment.

Hsieh's philosophy hinges on autonomy and has helped transform Zappos's customer service into an art form. The company repeatedly tops $1 billion in annual sales, with a majority of sales coming from repeat customers. They've managed to garner unprecedented loyalty from their consumers and are equally as beloved as an employer: since 2009, they've been listed on *Fortune*'s 100 Best Companies to Work For. There's no doubt in my mind that their success is a ripple effect that begins with Hsieh and the trust he imparts to his team.

There is little I can think of that's more fulfilling and, frankly, more *liberating* than giving over control to another capable person and watching him or her take the task or the team to a level you could not achieve yourself. There is also tremendous power in saying to another person, "Do what you think is best; I trust you." Just think of the pride of ownership you felt the last time someone said that to you.

Life

Our off-the-job life is often a testing ground for learning to trust others more, for it's in our personal lives that we're more likely to put down our armor, preconceptions, and defenses. In that world, who do you trust the most? What qualities do they possess that make it easier for you to hand over that trust? How does trust manifest in those relationships? Maybe it's a safe place to express your feelings, or a consistent showing of mutual respect for boundaries, or an opportunity to off-load tasks or chores to someone who you're confident will properly handle it. Regardless, doesn't it make you feel free when you're able to release that weight?

Now turn the mirror back on yourself. What qualities do you have that make people trust you? Are you able to earn it easily or do you see a pattern of people being wary of giving it to you? Despite our best intentions, letting others down is an inevitable occurrence. Are you quick to offer grace when trust is broken? Have you been shown that same forgiveness?

When it comes to our control issues, unpacking the relationship we have with trust is imperative. If we're looking for happy and fulfilling relationships in both our personal and professional lives, we must be ready and willing to trust others as well as ourselves and our own instincts; it's as much about self-awareness as it is about consideration, and it's the only way to build successful and meaningful partnerships.

Work

What's your collaboration style? Are you one of those people who's supposed to be working collectively with others but tends to hoard everything yourself? Or are you the type to sit back and let others take the reins while just waiting for your assignment? Working well as a team means knowing your own strengths and weaknesses and how they mesh or clash with those of your colleagues.

Some people want to take the credit and make sure they're being recognized for what they offer; they're more worried about themselves than the team's effort and its outcome. Then there are those who hardly contribute. They want to benefit from the hard work of others and use that success as a means to achieve their own; they ride the coattails, so to speak. Where do you fall? Are there situations and opportunities where you can ask for more control? Alternatively, where can you give it up and trust instead?

Leadership

Identify those in your company who have proven trustworthy already, the people whose competence and reliability make them your go-to colleagues. Are they being rewarded with more trust? Or do you feel that their proficiency is contingent on the short leash you have them on? If that's the case, is that a power play on your part or based on reality? Does that have to do with your limitations, or theirs?

If your company is improving in one area or another because of the people who are stewarding what they've been given, ask yourself if they're being rewarded for their individual contributions—whether that's verbally or monetarily, publicly or privately—or are you the one being rewarded for being a good leader? Who's reaping the benefits?

Behind every great leader is a great team, and the greatest leaders are the ones who recognize it. It's always important to remember that for the great achiever, it's all about "me." But for great leaders, it's all about "them."

CHAPTER 3

Harmony Enriches Most Any Tune

My first official leadership position was president of my middle school Boys' Glee Club. I'd been singing in the church choir for nearly ten years, so it made sense from that standpoint. What didn't make sense was how I got there. I was ushered into the position by the bully who pummeled me the week before. I quickly learned there was more to harmony than notes on paper.

Harmony is a funny thing. It's actually a pretty simple concept, defined musically as anytime you have multiple pitches being played at the same time. By strict definition, you can run your fingers along the strings of a guitar randomly, and no matter how beautiful or awful it sounds, technically it's a harmony. But I think we all know what the goal is when it comes to harmony—beautiful music. Few people pay money to hear discordant sound. We want to be moved by the beauty of complementary tones.

There were some absolutely incredible harmonies going on in the sixties and seventies, the golden era of music as far as my youth was concerned. I listened to a lot of music in those days, putting on a record whenever I could. Of course, it's not like today, when you can carry thousands of songs in your pocket or have virtually free access to the world's library of music. We had a record player in the house where someone was constantly spinning vinyl, from pop songs to show tunes, from Rachmaninov to Ray Stevens.

Then there was Steely Dan, which evolved to just two guys, Donald Fagen and Walter Becker. The aesthetic continuity of Steely Dan originated with those two, but they put out album after album with drums and bass and various guitarists and horns and other musicians. On a regular basis, Fagen and Becker had to think about who to bring in and how to produce the sound of the group with continuity. Talk about a situation that required recurring and deliberate harmony, both musically and relationally. As *Rolling Stone* put it after Walter Becker died in 2017, "Despite the ever-changing lineup, Steely Dan made their stamp on music with a string of pristine, sophisticated albums with 'calculated and literary lyrics' that blurred the lines of jazz, pop, rock, and soul."[7]

And then there was the legendary group the Mamas and the Papas. Michelle Phillips. Denny Doherty. John Phillips. And "Mama" Cass Elliot. When they first came on the scene in the late sixties, they set the music world buzzing. When

"California Dreamin'" was first released as a single, I didn't think I had ever heard anything like it before. The group's vocals were so tight, so precise, that they had an almost magical quality.

You know what I find fascinating? Their harmony, the sound of their different voices coming together created a thing all its own. Denny Doherty, the tenor of the group, described this "thing." And it was something all the band members experienced at one time or another when they sang: there were only four of them, but when they hit it just right, when they were all on their game and the notes were perfect, it actually sounded like a fifth voice was chiming in.

"When we were singing really well," explained Denny, "this phantom overtone voice would show up on top of everything else. It was a 'fifth' voice and we used to call it 'Harvey.'"

It wasn't really there, of course. They'd be singing, really close with their heads together trying to work on a part and suddenly they'd hear him and say, "Harvey's here!"

Denny went on to say, "Then it was like, 'OK, we can do it now. We found him!' When Harvey would appear, the arrangement would usually gel."[8]

Harvey. What a concept, that the perfect harmonization of multiple voices could lead to the creation of something entirely its own.

Of course, they didn't always coexist so harmonically. Anyone who knows the story of the Mamas and the Papas knows that their career together was painfully brief. Their short rise and fall included LSD trips, love triangles, splits and reunifications, and eventually "Mama" Cass Elliot's heart failure, the result of an overdose.

It seems that great, lasting harmonies among human beings are rare, whether we're talking musically or relationally. The ability for contrasting voices, in whatever field, to work together for extended periods of time is so unusual, because harmony, quite frankly, isn't easy.

Billy Joel, who has been performing for more than five decades and first became popular when I was growing up, knew that all too well. As a solo act, he didn't have the luxury of consonant vocal harmonies (though in his song "Through the Long Night," he harmonized with himself and accredited the inspiration to the Beatles' hit "Yes It Is.") But come 1987, he decided to experiment with an entirely different kind of harmony.

For as far back as I can remember, the prevailing political climate was the Cold War and the enemy was the Russians. In fact, in grade school we had air-raid drills where we would practice using the newly taught "duck and cover" as a method of personal protection against the effects of nuclear explosion (as if crouching under our desks was going to help anything).

Amid decades of the hostile power struggle between the Soviet Union and the U.S.-led Western powers, Billy Joel kept going back to a moment he saw on television from 1958 when an American pianist named Van Cliburn took part in a Russian piano competition—and won. Joel later said it had a huge impact on him, the realization that music transcended cultural and political lines, that a musician was capable of providing a moment of hope and warmth in the midst of the Cold War. So in the late eighties, after his album *The Bridge* was released, Joel decided to try for his own Van Cliburn moment.

Up until that point, rock music was not allowed in the USSR because it was not seen as part of Soviet culture. But in 1987, after Mikhail Gorbachev implemented glasnost—the Soviet policy of managed openness—Joel and his band traveled abroad to perform a total of six live concerts in Moscow and Leningrad. Joel brought along his family—his then-wife, supermodel Christie Brinkley, and their young daughter—as a way to show the Russian people that he trusted them and felt safe to bring his own loved ones into their environment. Before the concerts each night, Joel, his family, and his bandmates would spend their days interacting with the people of Russia, continually blown away at how hospitable and welcoming they were. On one of these outings they visited a monastery high up on a hill where a group of men performed hundred-year-old Georgian chants that were long believed to heal the sick. In an unplanned move, Joel joined in, interjecting some American doo-wop. The result was an impromptu concert that blended voices, styles, cultures, and human spirit.

What Billy Joel did on his Russian tour was groundbreaking—and not just the historical significance of going over there amid the tension-filled milieu (not to mention being one of the first American acts to play since the Berlin Wall went up). It was the sincerity he showed and the inclusiveness he demonstrated that set his visit apart. During one of his concerts, he introed the song "Allentown" by saying, "This song is about young people living in the Northeast of America. Their lives are miserable because the steel factories are closing. They desperately want to leave but they stay because they were brought up to believe that things were going to get better . . . maybe that sounds familiar." Through Joel's empathy and utter humanity, everybody in the room became part of the same message.

Years later, Joel reflected back on the trip and said, "The trip to Russia was probably the biggest highlight for me as a performer . . . I met these people and they weren't the enemy . . . What happens when your kid says to you, 'What did you do in the Cold War, Daddy?' And now we have something to say."[9]

He headed to Russia as a rock-and-roll musician and left as a symbol of connection. Not long after, the Berlin Wall came down and the communist party was kicked out. There were a lot of dynamics going on at that time, but who's to say that Billy Joel's visit didn't contribute to these dramatic changes? Who's to say that the freedom and solidarity of his presence didn't permanently affect the country and play a role in the ultimate dissolution of the USSR in 1991?

What would happen if we all took such an active role in creating harmony?

Harmony has a lot to teach us about leadership and coexisting with others. Whether it's in the workplace, government, personal relationships, or the world in general, we are constantly required to figure out new ways to blend our various "voices" with those around us, and hopefully in ways that are mutually beneficial.

I didn't start realizing that until my Glee Club presidency stint. At that age, I thought harmony only pertained to music, that it was only important as far as musical chords and voice ranges were concerned. But my perspective started to shift when I was put in charge of the class when the teacher was out. Getting dysfunctional boys to sing functionally together, in harmony, is one thing. It's quite another when you're expected to keep the peace among those dysfunctional boys.

That lesson sank deeper the following year during my first year of high school. All I knew was that integration—the attempt to merge people together—had to be better than shrugging my shoulders and leaving them to argue from opposite sides of the room.

• • •

WHEN I BEGAN my career at Sonic, I was struck by the disharmony within the system. In fact, you could describe it as downright dysfunctional. It wasn't that we sang together poorly; we often could not even agree on a tune.

Whenever the franchisor would recommend going a certain direction, many of the franchisees would do just the opposite. When our company announced we had selected

Coca-Cola as the primary cola vendor and negotiated new marketing benefits to the relationship, a couple of franchise groups immediately went to Pepsi-Cola and negotiated a multiyear supply contract for their group of stores. When the franchisor announced that we were going to be utilizing a single creative agency, a group of Houston franchisees and their agency sued us, seeking to advertise independently from the system.

In the 1980s, the Sonic system was filled with this kind of discordant behavior. The first leadership challenge was to get them to want to harmonize at all, let alone come up with a new set of tunes.

Disharmony was sure to hold our businesses back. At the time I became COO of Sonic in 1993, we had begun to negotiate with our franchise leadership for a new, system-wide license agreement. I was convinced that we needed to include an array of new contractual requirements, obligating our operators to comply with more of a single system. It was difficult to see how we could help them from a volume-purchasing and cost-saving standpoint otherwise, much less build a consistent and coherent system for our customers' sake.

The negotiation process itself was somewhat disharmonious. Late in the process, our franchise leadership began attacking our CEO publicly concerning issues under negotiation. Unbeknown to our franchise leadership, our CEO was ready to throw in the towel. Fortunately, several others of us had begun to "sing the same tune," so we had no interest in turning back. Our new agreement obligated all franchisees, among other things, to utilize a single advertising agency, selected by the franchisor; purchase food and paper goods contracted for by the franchisor; utilize a single cola vendor; utilize a consistent menu; and upgrade the trade dress of their buildings at least once every seven years.

In exchange for this, we offered our operators newly extended terms, up to twenty years, and greater trade radius—physical space around their stores in which a new store could not be built—for protection of their business growth.

While the prior negotiation process was not harmonious, 90+ percent of the stores eligible to convert to this new license agreement elected to do so. In one last gap of disharmony, though, our franchise operators wanted to delay the date of implementation, claiming challenges with the amount of paperwork involved; we agreed to delay the paperwork due date, but only with the retroactive application of the new agreements' economics to the previous September 1.

We had not yet learned how to sing together, but finally we were working on the same tune.

The consequences of this "harmonization" process increased Sonic's buying power and delivered substantial savings to our franchisees. The introduction of a consistent menu across our franchises gave us the opportunity to promote new products. We were able to deploy increased store-level profits toward new advertising, product promotions, and new store development beyond any historical level.

In a five-year period from 1996 to 2001, annual aggregate

profits for our restaurant operators increased by more than $100 million. We were finally making beautiful music together.

• • •

WHEN I THINK of leaders who understood the potential power of harmony applied on a global basis, Woodrow Wilson certainly is one who comes to mind. He pursued unusually grand goals in his life, in an attempt to achieve global cooperation. And though he since has become known to have held harsh racial views even worse than may have been common at the time, his biography quotes him in 1880 as having said "because I love the South, I rejoice in the failure of the confederacy." Like many, his was a flawed character, full of contradictions.

Wilson was an educated man, having graduated with a Ph.D. from John Hopkins University in history and political science. He was eventually brought on as the president of Princeton, but once he was there he felt the elitism and casual standards were wreaking havoc, so he tried to tackle those problems—only to bang up against a brutal Princeton hierarchy pretty intent on keeping things as they were. This unharmonious situation provoked him to enter politics.

Wilson's political career grew serious when he ran for governor of New Jersey in 1910, and he quickly parlayed his growing reputation to gain the Democratic nomination for the presidency in 1912. Which he won. He could have used his quick ascension to squash those around him, but instead he was constantly reaching out, constantly searching for common ground, constantly trying to harmonize various aspects of the world with one another.

As the years passed, his deep reticence to join World War I was eroded by Germany's "unrestricted submarine warfare." Eventually, rumors that Germany might help Mexico advance into the southern United States convinced him to ask Congress to declare war, a request that was overwhelmingly supported by the government. By November of 1918, Germany was defeated.

This is when Woodrow Wilson began to pursue worldwide harmony in earnest, meeting with the victorious Allies and presenting his famous Fourteen Points speech. His aim? Nothing short of a lasting world peace. He had seen what world war could do, and he was determined to work with other leaders to set a world stage where war would never happen again, at least not on that scale. Wilson spoke on behalf of renouncing secret treaties, recognizing the principles of self-determination, removing tariff barriers, reducing arms levels, and introducing a group that could arbitrate disputes: the League of Nations.

But the Allies were reluctant to sign anything that might jeopardize their colonial structure and interests, and a U.S. Congress, weary of war and world involvement, preferred to remain isolated from European issues. Again, Wilson proved to have an enormous amount of foresight when he said, "I can predict with absolute certainty that within another generation there will be another world war if the nations of the world do not concert the method by which to prevent it."

As we all know now, he was right.

In music and in life, the strength of harmony is never so apparent as when you see the weaknesses that occur when harmony breaks down. Lack of harmony causes all kinds of discordant sounds and strife, but harmony can actually create this "other" presence that individuals and teams working in isolation from each other can never achieve

Conflict, though, is inevitable. No matter who or where, there will always be clashing personalities, differing sides of the story, opposing beliefs, and societal upheaval. It's a question of when, not what. I keep in my back pocket the reminder that compassion and communication can go a long way in the face of discord. They can't always lead to resolution, but to liken it back to music, if there is more than one note to be played simultaneously, we have to at least attempt to play together.

There are limits, however, to what a leader or groups of leaders can achieve, particularly when participants cannot handle new challenges. The great recession of 2008 provided just this test for some members of the Sonic system. Unfortunately, some franchisees could not rise to the challenge. They became increasingly discordant over the next two to three years and we had to make the decision to remove them from their stores. While it was a painful process, it was necessary in order to preserve companywide harmony.

When times get tough, it may be necessary to throw some of the weaker "singers" out of the system in order to preserve harmony (value). That's the leader's job too: not just to make harmony possible to achieve, but also to recognize when the group's coherence and harmony is threatened—and to fix it.

As leader of the Glee Club and later as a leader at Sonic, I began to learn that the duty of anyone seeking to lead is, at its core, an exercise in understanding, inclusion, and harmony. Leading cannot be about stealing the show or imprinting your authority on everything you touch. It cannot focus on differences over commonalities, or antipathy over camaraderie. The true leader mirrors the leader of a great band and is always trying to figure out ways to bring together otherwise discordant voices. Because ultimately, without harmony, life would consist of only one melody without any accompaniment. And who in their right mind would want to live like that?

RULE OF THUMB #3:
Harmony Requires Contrast and Multiple Voices.

I was fresh out of law school when I joined a firm in Baltimore to try my hand at corporate law. And while I'm sure that that legal niche at that particular firm was fulfilling for some people, I wasn't one of them. I was green and had my sights set on changing the world as an attorney. I was full of big ideas and even bigger ideals, and what I walked into was not the type of atmosphere that was going to foster such a mentality.

When I look back on it now, it's clear that my distaste for the whole experience wasn't about the field of practice but about the environment. When I went to work every day during that first year of my employment, what I found was an old boys' network, a real every-man-for-himself type of arrangement. It seemed like a race for who could outwork, outsmart, or outargue the guy sitting next to him. If I were to put that in musical terms, it would be cacophony, a discordant mixture of sounds. All it seemed to be was a lot of noise—a loud racket—and it wasn't pretty to listen to.

Have you ever been in an environment like that? As if you're part of a symphony full of musicians among whom no two have the same sheet of music in front of them? It seemed that no matter what I did or how hard I tried to rationalize it to myself, there was no way to get the contrasting voices of myself, my coworkers, and my superiors to blend together. That's when I sought a different soundtrack for my life and ultimately came to find that there was greater opportunity for harmony in the corporate environment. At Sonic, I found a similar diversity of voices, but not everyone was bent on playing their tune over the top of everyone else's. It was in this sort of environment that I thrived in my own career and then, when I was in a position to do so, gave others opportunities to thrive in theirs.

Claudia San Pedro is a fine example of this. She was born

in Mexico City and her family moved to Baltimore, Maryland, around the time she was two years old, eventually settling in Norman, Oklahoma, when she was five. By 2004, perhaps in her mid-thirties, she was managing the office of the state budget, overseeing a $6 billion annual operating budget for the State of Oklahoma. I'd met her through a state nonprofit organization focused on policy development and was very impressed with her. I spent some time getting to know her and attempting to recruit her to join Sonic. In 2006, she agreed to do so and came on board as our treasurer and vice president of investor relations. A couple of years later, I added strategic planning to her responsibilities, which permitted her to join the senior management team and participate in planning discussions ongoing. This was a key factor in her professional development and, without question, in the growth of the company.

In 2015, she became CFO of Sonic, and in January 2018, she became president of our franchising company, Sonic Industries. When I departed the company in December 2018, she was made president of the Sonic companies that folded into Inspire Brands. Claudia represented well the scope of opportunity, no matter one's gender or ethnicity, that our company had become known for to such a degree that the *New York Times* recognized the fact, calling our leadership "a rarity in corporate America—a management team that is mostly women and minorities and a board that is close to that."[10] The value I had gained as a teenager open to gender and ethnic variety had taken root over time at Sonic.

Life

Is the cadence of your home life smooth and harmonious, or does it sound more like a lot of voices talking (or maybe screaming) at once? What about the people who make up your inner circle, whether that's a spouse and children or friends and extended family? Is there an understanding that everybody has an instrument to play and can be evenly heard? Or do you need to determine the rules of who plays their instrument when, and then figure out the roles of who leads the chorus, and who, if any, is the designated conductor? Oftentimes, harmony can be achieved by simply gaining clarity about who's responsible for what part.

The needs, goals, and strengths of every individual will always be varied. Some people have rhythm, some are tone deaf, and some are prodigies, but despite those inevitable differences, everyone deserves to feel like they have a voice; to feel like their instrument matters. Instead of tuning them out or swapping them out for a smaller solo, you may just have to orchestrate it differently.

Work

When you're on the job, what's the soundtrack playing in your headphones? Is your daily grind spent listening to diverse music and voices, or do you hear the same song over and over again? If you're listening to one song on repeat, I'd venture to say you're slowly driving yourself crazy. It may be the reason you're unhappy with your job. In fact, it may be the reason that a reported 71 percent of U.S. workers are unhappy with their jobs and looking to change employers.[11]

Harmony at work doesn't mean that everyone is singing to a prescribed tune. Rather, it means that every person has their own pitch, but when put together, they all sing their parts and form a cohesive ensemble. It means people are working individually but operating collectively; if and when they're not working on the same projects, they're working on projects that have a common goal. Do the individuals who are working on various points within a project understand how their part plays a role in the song's final cut?

Leadership

The soundtrack of your organization is the culture that perpetuates from the top down. As a leader, what would your people say is the music playing in the overhead speaker while they work? Is it boring elevator music, or inspiring tunes from the *Rocky IV* soundtrack, or hard rock that gets people fired up, or calming jazz that's heavy on horns? Based on the daily setlist that you spread through the airwaves, what sentiments are people consistently receiving from you?

Everyone has different tastes, and embracing those differences is what makes a more eclectic, rich, and melodious soundtrack. Therefore, compiling a medley may be in order: a beautiful symphony where the anxious find solace, heavy metal that tests the patience (and sanity) of those who are averse to chaos, classic blues so the overly caffeinated are encouraged to relax. In the midst of ever-clashing needs, being a well-rounded leader who intentionally helps people learn and grow will more likely achieve a harmonious environment where all genres are welcome.

CHAPTER 4

Just Say Yes

By the spring of 1989, as the general counsel at Sonic, I was convinced that I needed to start looking for other employment options. I had been working closely with the company CEO through our 1988 recapitalization, but I began to get the vibe that the COO, a fellow named Vern Stewart, felt that I had outlived my usefulness to him. He had done a masterful job at bringing in some new blood, improving our marketing fund, and ultimately driving traffic to our locations. He was tough, to say the least. Actually, to be completely truthful, he was a shrewd character, somewhat Napoleonic, and after I had finished my work on the recapitalization, he seemed finished with me.

I started putting out some feelers at other companies. I wondered where I might land next. The oil bust had hit our region hard in the eighties, and by the spring of '89 I might have had more money than I had ever had before, but there weren't a ton of jobs out there. I had a wife in graduate school and a three-year-old son to take care of. Regardless, I had my ear to the ground for a new opportunity.

Then came one of those unexpected twists of fate. Vern Stewart was summarily fired—I won't go into the details here—and with that move, the operation of the company was scattered to the wind. Our new partners—51 percent owners of the company—made it abundantly clear that there was one reason they were comfortable investing in Sonic, and that reason was Vern Stewart. They told me they were stunned at his sudden departure, no matter the reason, and six months after he was fired, their point man, Jack Donahue, called and said that at the next management retreat, they wanted to discuss going public—undoubtedly so they could liquidate their ownership. Jack wanted me to head up the discussion of the process at that retreat.

So, in March of 1990, that's exactly what I did. I did my homework, spoke with other companies that had gone public, and tried to lay out a plan. By the summer of 1990, we selected investment bankers, and by September of the same year, we filed with the SEC the necessary papers for a public stock offering. This was only weeks before Saddam Hussein invaded Kuwait. Our offering was then delayed by a lousy stock market, until the U.S. invaded Iraq in January 1991 and Iraq ended its invasion of Kuwait. With this turn of events, the market turned north and so did our stock offering in February 1991.

What a crazy time. I went from thinking I was finished at the company to having some breathing room to overseeing Sonic going public. Talk about experiencing innovation on a very personal level—my role was constantly changing in those days, based on whatever project landed in front of me. We went public in 1991 at $12.50 a share, and by all accounts the whole thing was a huge success. Five years before, a group of Sonic leaders, myself included, had hurriedly bought the company for $10 million (more on that later) and now it was valued at ten times that. On paper, I became a millionaire. After Sonic became a public company, I felt like I'd worked hard and been well rewarded, but I simultaneously felt rising uncertainty. I never saw myself in corporate America. I had history and law degrees, not an M.B.A. In fact, before Sonic I had no corporate experience and especially not in a leadership position. I'd suddenly made enough money—at least on paper—to take a break and think about what I might like to do next, but that was unappealing. I was still young and I liked having something to do. Besides, I already knew I didn't have an answer for what was next. Largely because I never planned to be where I was in the first place. I'd just kept saying yes.

In 1992, the answer came. My boss offered me the position of CFO, an opportunity that required the development of a completely new skill set, so I literally said, "Yeah, why not?" I had gained an on-the-job education in corporate finance and was now being asked to put it to work full-time. These new challenges kept me busy for a time, but by the spring of 1993, I was ready for something new and different, so I went to my boss and gave him six months' notice. I planned on leaving by the end of the year, approaching my ten-year anniversary with Sonic, and I was afraid that if I didn't put in my notice with them, I'd end up hanging around long past my usefulness.

But ninety days later, my boss came to me again, asking if I would consider moving into the COO position. And again, I thought it would be a good opportunity to learn some new stuff, so I said, "Yeah, why not?!" In August of 1993, I was promoted to COO, and in 1994, president.

Then came the board meeting in April of 1995, a meeting that would put me on a new and even more challenging trajectory. None of the independent board members, nor I, had any idea what was about to happen. But as we sat there at the meeting, the CEO stood up, told everyone he was accepting a position at another company, and he had a car waiting outside to take him to the airport, where a private plane awaited him. Thank you very much and good-bye.

He was gone.

Sonic did not have a CEO.

The collective faces of the board of Sonic swiveled around, looked at me, and one of them asked me to leave the room. I did. But what a weird moment. Stunned at my former boss's news, I stood outside wondering what was next . . . but not for long. Our board called me back into the boardroom and asked if I wanted to be the CEO of Sonic. I engaged in a short calculation and said, "Yeah, why not?!" And so began my twenty three-year run as CEO of a public company called Sonic.

• • •

THERE'S SOMEONE IN the business world who has become the king of saying yes, known far and wide for his willingness to do or try anything, and I mean anything. In 1986 he crossed the Atlantic in a boat in world-record time, crushing the previous mark. At one point he took a leap off a casino in Las Vegas. He kite-surfed across the English Channel. And he goes jet-skiing in his tuxedo.[12]

But he doesn't limit his risk-taking to personal endeavors. He has also had his fingers in just about every industry you can think of, from clothing to music to airlines to space travel. It's gone so far that his nickname among his employees throughout his worldwide company is "Doctor Yes."

Of course, you probably know I'm talking about Richard Branson, the high school dropout and eventual founder of the Virgin empire.

"Even if I have no idea where I'm going or how to get there, I prefer to say yes instead of no," he wrote on his blog. "Opportunity favors the bold."

Saying yes won't always work out the way you hoped. When Branson tried to cross the Pacific Ocean in a hot-air balloon in 1991 with a copilot, he didn't end up in his targeted location of Los Angeles, California. He actually landed in the Arctic. And after he said yes to participating in the Virgin Strive Challenge—an event in which a team of athletes went from the base of the Matterhorn to the top of Mount Etna completely under human power—he hit an unexpected speed bump in the dark while going downhill at full speed, flying over the handlebars. Some of his yeses have led to life-threatening situations. But all of his yeses have taught him something or given him an experience he never would have had otherwise.

Saying yes doesn't always end well. A life in which you say yes is not usually a pain-free life. Saying yes will not lead to a comfortable life where you follow the same routine day in and day out. "Yes" is a disruptive word, a risky word, the kind of word that leads you into new directions.

This is why saying yes is such an amazing way to live a life.

When I talk about saying yes (and I think this lines up with Branson's take), I'm talking about maintaining a willingness to embark on whatever path that's in front of you with curiosity and a willingness to give it your best shot. This doesn't mean you say yes in a way that leads to a chaotic life, and it doesn't mean you say yes to doing things you know you hate doing. If someone asks me if I will do their taxes for them, that's going to be a "No." I don't enjoy filling out the 1040, and my life is busy enough without taking on someone else's busywork.

The kind of opportunities I'm talking about are the ones

that arouse your curiosity, that have you sitting back and thinking, "Huh, that's interesting. Maybe we should give this a try." Even when they don't at first make sense.

A perfect example of this with Branson is what happened when he and his future wife, Joan, were on their way to Puerto Rico, only to discover their flight was canceled. The two of them found themselves stuck at a small island airport with hundreds of other passengers, all of whom were angry, tired, and frustrated that they weren't able to go home. What did Branson do? Sit it out in the airport? Wait for another flight? Tell jokes in the waiting area?

This is Sir Richard Branson we're talking about. He decided to charter his own plane.

Branson tracked down a charter plane that would hold all of the passengers and then offered them a seat at cost: the amount he had to pay for the plane divided by the number of passengers. Everyone paid him $39, and they were off. It wasn't long after that when an acquaintance came to him with the idea of starting an international airline, and Branson said—what else would Doctor Yes say?—yes.

And that's not even the only airline Branson started on a kind of whim. In his autobiography, *Finding My Virginity*, he talks about how disappointed he was when one of his chief financial officers made the difficult decision to step away from Virgin so that he could move home with his family to Australia. Beyond the disappointment, though, Branson was happy for the man, Brett Godfrey, and wished him all the best. As he hung up the phone, he told Godfrey to stay in touch and let him know if there were any business opportunities in Australia.

Godfrey immediately told Branson about an idea he had for a low-cost airline in Australia. Branson was interested. He asked Godfrey for a more detailed plan. Godfrey had a plan to him the next morning. This quick exchange, one that happened off the cuff, one that Branson simply said yes to, ended up becoming Virgin Australia.

"Life is a lot more fun when you say yes!" Branson said. "It's amazing how that one little word can lead you on an incredible adventure."

This willingness to try just about anything was something that began early on in his life. Branson dropped out of school in his early teens. He said he was thought to be "the dumbest person at school." (Only later did he learn he was dyslexic.) But this is when he decided to create *Student* magazine. He had revolutionary ideas he wanted to write about that the school paper wouldn't dare publish, thoughts about music and the Vietnam War. And he started by listing names, costs, and potential advertisers in a small notebook. The only problem? He had no money to put toward it.

But he moved forward anyway. This is the beautiful thing about saying yes: even when you don't have a plan mapped out, even when you're not sure what to do next, saying yes gives you momentum, it keeps you moving forward.

Saying yes will sometimes even summon fate. Or so it seems, at least in Branson's story, because it was at about that time that his mother found an expensive necklace on the ground close to their home. She turned it in to the police, but after a certain time passed without anyone claiming it, they returned it to her. She sold it for 100 pounds, gave her son the money, and Branson, along with his young business partner, used the money to pay off their magazine's bills and keep the operation afloat.[13]

Within a few years, Branson capitalized on the growing success of his magazine and started a mail-order record business that would eventually become Virgin Records.

"That 100 pounds ended up paving the way for Virgin Galactic, Virgin Atlantic, and all the other Virgin companies around the world today," writes Branson.

What opportunities are presenting themselves to you right now that you should be saying yes to?

It makes me think about improvisational comedy. In an improv group, members ask for audience suggestions, and then use those suggestions to create a skit. It's spontaneous, unpredictable, and extremely amusing to watch. Improvisation seems incredibly difficult since people appear to be making up an entire skit on the spot. But, upon close inspection, it turns out that improvisation isn't as random as it appears. Sure, when comedic actors are in the high-stakes situation of a performance, they act quickly and make snap judgments, but they also follow certain rules.

The basis of improv's spontaneity is the "yes, and" rule: when a performer offers a suggestion or new idea, the other performers immediately agree with the idea and use it to move the scene forward, to build upon each new contribution.

What's important to realize here is that the "yes, and" rule doesn't offer any advice for *what* to do or say in an improv performance; rather it creates the optimal *conditions* for a good performance. It sets the stage for agility and creativity. "Yes, and" creates, while "no" would stop the flow.

This isn't just a good lesson for life, but also applicable in the corporate world. In fact, improvisational comedy workshops have become a staple at business schools. A businessman by the name of Bob Kulhan, who drew on his experience performing on the Chicago sketch comedy scene, partnered with a professor at Duke University's Fuqua School of Business to launch an improv training program tailored to M.B.A. students.[14] The program focuses on using improv as an exercise in team building and problem-solving, and has since expanded to the business schools at universities like UCLA, Columbia, and Indiana.

Hesitant? After all, humor and comedic timing aren't often the first things that come to mind when people think about their place of work. But think of it this way: "yes, and" can be the antidote to workplace negativity. There is safety in saying no, but saying yes—even if just for a moment—can create the opportunity to follow an idea and see where it goes.

• • •

OF COURSE, AS soon as I start talking about saying yes, about remaining open to change, the question inevitably arises:

How do you say yes to things without walking away from your existing commitments? Doesn't a culture of saying yes lead to a kind of flakiness where you're changing your mind every other day?

The short answer is, no, a culture of yes doesn't mean you are constantly changing your mind. This is how I see it.

First, I think that it's important that your entire team is aligned behind a series of big-picture initiatives, and broadly this would mean strategic initiatives as part of a business plan. These must remain clear and at the forefront of everyone's mind, because if these main initiatives are not clarified in the beginning, individual team members can easily begin to wander; before you know it, the whole team is wandering here and there and everywhere. This compromises accountability and invites a culture in which alterations are constantly being made. A team simply cannot be effective if their target is constantly moving.

If your plan is based on certain activities (meetings or exchanges) but not initiatives, these kinds of slipping alterations can easily occur—with no main objectives, no tactics or activities are seen as being more valuable than others. A strategic plan must include key initiatives that will drive the plan—this keeps the team aligned and focused, and it ensures that their efforts are driving progress and not just busywork. If you have a team that buys into these key initiatives, then you're all set.

Now, of course, new ideas will always arise, especially if your team is filled with curious people. And you want curious people. But a team with an aligned strategic focus will always approach new ideas with the right questions: What is the objective of the new idea? How does that objective align with our original initiatives? Who are the right people to get behind this new objective?

If the plan aligns completely but also provides a better mousetrap, then by all means, alter your original plan. But if it is simply a stimulating idea with no alignment to your original initiatives, then you should probably jettison it—unless you are prepared to do the heavy lifting of overhauling your entire set of initiatives.

This is a major filter I use for new ideas and for trying to figure out if "yes" is the right answer to the question. This can help your team maintain the energy that comes with saying yes while keeping everyone aligned, focused, and as productive as they can be.

In my opinion, saying yes is the precursor to variety. I've made no secret of my love of variation, which might seem odd considering I held the same position at Sonic for over two decades. But it's important to remember that variety isn't limited to *what* you do; it can easily pertain to *how* you it.

When Walt Disney was making the movie *Bambi*, in order to draw realistic-looking animals, he hired an expert on anatomy to teach the animators. In on-site art classes at Hyperion Studios, animators spent months concentrating on drawing four-footed creatures both small and large, working off of instruction sheets that showcased deer anatomy and movement structure. When Disney wanted the drawings to be even more lifelike, he paid photographers to go out into the Maine wilderness to capture scenes of deer and rabbits in their natural habitat to give to the animators to study.

Then, wanting to go one step further, Disney created a small zoo on the studio lot and brought in two young fawns so the animators could observe the animals directly. That way, they could not only see the deer up close, but also feel them. In the book *Disney Animation: The Illusion of Life*, the authors write, "Nothing matches the learning that comes from feeling an animal's bones and muscles and joints, to discover how they are put together and how far they can move in any direction; it is always surprising."[15] But then animators really showed their dedication to the craft when they observed a deer corpse in various stages of decomposition in order to see how the muscles and tendons worked at the cellular level.

To give animators the best chance at producing the best product, Disney used various tactics to inspire his team. Can you imagine how mundane it would have been for Disney to assign a task—draw a deer—and then spend months not being satisfied yet not offering his artists anything more to go on? Ingenuity requires variety. That was certainly the case here—compared to earlier animation, *Bambi* was groundbreaking in its realism; it created an entirely new standard.

Are there new ways you could look at something?

What different strides could you take to produce the best outcome?

How could you infuse variety in solving the next problem that comes across your desk?

• • •

LONG BEFORE RICHARD Branson showed the world how powerful saying yes could be, there was another adventurous spirit who set the bar. Back in the thirteenth century, a boy named Marco Polo was born in Venice, Italy. He was fifteen years old when he first met his father and uncle, who were traveling jewel merchants returning to Venice after a long voyage. They wasted no time in planning their next trip, this time asking seventeen-year-old Marco to go with them. He said yes.

The three Polos traveled throughout Asia for the next twenty-four years—yes, you read that right. From the Middle East to Pakistan to Beijing, from the Chinese port of Amoy (now known as Xiamen) back to the Persian Gulf, they explored territories on foot, horseback, and later, by ship. A couple years into their trek, they arrived at the court of Kublai Khan—the ruler of the Mongol Empire and founder of the Yuan dynasty, who was an earlier acquaintance of Marco's father and uncle. Khan took a liking to the youngest Polo and employed him as a special envoy of the Chinese monarch, sending him on special missions throughout China, Burma (now Myanmar), and India. So obscure were some of these specific locations, they were not seen again by Europeans until last century.[16]

Over the span of two decades, Polo traversed thousands of miles. He endured illness and famine, made his way through uncharted deserts and steep mountain passes, and survived extreme weather and the wrath of wild animals. Along the way, he became the governor of a Chinese city, was appointed as an official of the Privy Council, and even tried his hand as a tax inspector in the city of Yanzhou. He navigated numerous different cultures with apparent ease, became fluent in four different languages, and upon his return to Venice, is said to be responsible for introducing Europeans to the compass, paper, porcelain, ivory, jade, spices, and paper money.

What's remarkable about Marco Polo isn't that he was the first European to explore Asia—he wasn't—but that he was the first to document it. His book, *The Travels of Marco Polo*, came out around the year 1300 (though about 140 years shy of the printing press so they were hand-copied manuscripts) and provided detailed accounts of his routes, impressions, and experiences. His work gave readers a new view of the world, opened up new possibilities for trade and exploration, and even today is widely considered to be "the most influential travelogue ever written." [17]

All because he said yes. He had no idea where the road was going to take him. He didn't narrow his focus to one place, one outcome, or even one language. He just kept moving forward, kept saying yes, kept embracing the variety of the unknown. This insatiable curiosity gave him not only a very storied life, but a permanent spot in world history.

RULE OF THUMB #4:
Say Yes and Then Figure It Out.

In 2007 the Media Lab at MIT conducted a study[18] where they fitted students with custom-made electronic "black boxes" to monitor them as they went about their day—working, meeting, eating, going out, and sleeping. The devices recorded where they went and how fast, their tone of voice, and subtle details about their body language. What it revealed is that a good 90 percent of what people do in any day follows routines so complete that their behavior can be predicted with just a few mathematical equations.

Our brains are hardwired for predictability. Whether it's a daily habit, driving a specific route, or reacting to something in a customary way, we tend to be creatures of habit and stick with what we know. But why is that? Evolutionary psychology holds that although we currently inhabit a thoroughly modern world of technology, space exploration, and virtual realities, we do so with the ingrained mentality of Stone Age hunter-gatherers. That is, people today still seek the traits that made survival possible back then: an instinct to fight furiously when threatened, for instance, or an innate drive to trade information and share secrets.

Some things never change, which could be because of our nature, but there are plenty of other instances where we consciously choose to live on autopilot; we choose familiarity because it feels safest. We get locked into a routine and stay there, unwilling to explore, because we're just trying to survive. But the point of modern life isn't about surviving; it's about thriving. What would happen if you decided to break free from the familiar and go beyond survival? What would your world look like if you opted for the unpredictable route and chose to thrive?

Life

Relationships are one of the areas where we are most naturally resistant to variety, the areas in which we are most naturally inclined to routine. We see the same people, talk to the same people, and trust the same people. While people are one of the greatest gifts we have in life, why limit that blessing to the select few we already know?

Do you remember going to summer camp when you were a kid? What did you feel like when you first arrived? If you were like me, there was a dash of excitement mixed with a gallon of anxiety. The anxiety was all about one thing: there were a ton of other kids I didn't know. Now consider how it always felt at the end of that summer camp. You were probably on one of the greatest highs in life. In fact, the people you were so anxious about meeting had become such good friends that you were probably holding back tears as you packed your bags and said good-bye!

When it comes to new relationships, we can hesitate like a kid going to camp or we can add variety to our repertoire and remember that the most rewarding part of camp was never the activities, it was the rich friendships with people you would have likely never met otherwise. I know many adults who still count friends they met at camp as some of their very best friends in life.

Work

Consider what elements of your workday, or career in general, have become uninspiring and even boring. Get specific. Is it the cramped desk? The lack of view? The monotonous tasks? Now consider your approach to those elements. Is there anything in your power that you can do to spice things up?

I'm not saying that if you're bored at work you should up and change jobs, but I am saying that there are some easy things you can do to introduce variety to help ease the taedium vitae. What if you spent part of your workday standing at your desk instead of sitting? The position in which we work is an underappreciated component that can have a massive effect, much bigger than the change itself. What if you opted to work remotely for a couple hours or days a week? A change of scenery, whether it's at home or in a café, can inject new vibrance into your day. What if you decided to tackle that dreaded daily task in the afternoon instead of the morning? Maybe you could listen to music while doing it and experiment with different bands to see who makes it feel the most enjoyable.

Don't be afraid of change, especially not small change. In a business environment, making an incremental shift in the way things are typically done does not significantly threaten existing power structures or alter current methods. Focus on the small, daily investments that may soon lead to big results.

Leadership

We are living in the most constantly changing work environment in our lifetimes, thanks to the prevailing force of technology. This isn't the era to become a slave to strict rules and procedures. But as a CEO, I know certain protocols are needed in order to be efficient—especially if you're leading a larger organization. Therefore, if the "what" needs to remain the same, move to more variety in the "how."

If a customer is unhappy about a product they received, there is likely a protocol in place that ensures how the company can try to make the customer happy without losing money. That's the "what" and often includes things like pushing #9 to receive a return label followed by the issuance of store credit within seven to ten business days. A lot of companies have that buttoned up and they don't want to change it. Maybe what can change, or the way variety can be introduced, is in "how" it's carried out.

Tony Hsieh introduced a new "how" by making sure Zappos customers always talk to a live person who has the freedom and flexibility to exercise their best judgment. One such instance was when a female customer called trying to return some boots. It turned out she bought them for her father, who had since died. The Zappos customer service rep told her not to bother returning them; they would refund her money and she was free to give the boots away instead of sending them back. After the call, the rep sent her some flowers. Sometime after that, she sent the rep a letter and a photo of her father.

In reimagining the "how," Hsieh not only engendered trust in the people and made his company's brand extremely well known and well loved; he actually made his customer service department highly efficient.

The first question we should ask as leaders today is, where is our routine making us incapable of quick change? The second question is, how can we keep our "how" in a state of flexibility?

CHAPTER 5

You Don't Need to Originate Opportunities to Seize Them

Sometimes the best opportunities take planning, forethought, and salesmanship, coming after months of hard work that eventually culminates in a done deal, a signed contract, or a new partnership. These kinds of hard-fought battles are very rewarding. They give you a sense of control and self-worth and a little boost in confidence.

At other times, opportunity will come up out of nowhere, even bite you in the butt. In these cases, you probably didn't do much to plan or prepare for it. You didn't strategize or try to outmaneuver someone else. All you did was work hard, kept doing what you were doing, and when the opportunity showed itself, you weaved it into your own plan—or even made it your plan.

Let me introduce you to someone who almost singlehandedly changed my life (though he may not have intended it), someone whose actions stirred up a huge opportunity for me: his name was Jim Barrett. He was one of my earliest contacts at Sonic—I had met him through my parents, years before, in my late teens. He was not only an officer in the company, he was also a stockholder, a board member, and a franchisee, owning over thirty stores. He was doing very well financially and had a law degree from American University in Washington, D.C. He had worked in the Washington offices of the late U.S. senator Robert S. Kerr, and perhaps something of that city had rubbed off on him: he was clever and tenacious.

By the time I joined the company in 1984, Barrett was no longer an officer or on the board of directors, but he was still a stockholder in Sonic and he still owned all his stores. Because of how I understood his departure from the company was handled, I believed by then he had a bit of a chip on his shoulder.

It was ironic that I attended a meeting Barrett requested, probably early in 1985—after all, I had barely turned thirty, was relatively new to the company, and just trying to keep my head above water and learn as much as I could. My boss was thirty-six years old, so we were both pretty wet behind the ears. Barrett was my parents' age, maybe in his mid-fifties, and he walked into the room with his lawyer, whom I immediately recognized. In fact, I had known his attorney for nearly fifteen years, having first met him in community activities, then working for him at a restaurant he owned while I was in college, and then having him write one of my recommendations for law school when I applied to Georgetown Law. So, there I was, the youngest one in the group, but also the only one who knew everyone else. This might have left me relaxed, but instead I was pretty much on edge.

Barrett dove right in. He was unhappy about everything, and he made a surprising threat: he said he was going to buy the company. He would go out and talk to the three hundred shareholders, convince enough of them to sell to him, and then he'd come back with control of the company, fire us all, shut down the overhead, and begin running it as the franchisor. The company would be his. I remember sitting there listening to him, and I was completely stunned. I don't think any of us had seen that coming. I mean, he was often unhappy about something, but not to the extent that he would talk about a hostile takeover of the company and firing everyone.

Well, our CEO was as shocked as I was. Barrett was kind of a Wile E. Coyote, so it was impossible to tell precisely how serious he was, but there was some legitimate concern that he might pull this off and take over Sonic. If there was a chance to buy the company, senior management was interested and, more important, given the oil bust environment at the time, none of us wanted to lose our jobs. As soon as the meeting ended, my boss was on the phone with the founder and the board, which was well within his responsibility.

Our founder, Troy Smith, alarmed at the idea of Barrett's potential takeover and wanting to head off the same, went to his friends who were stockholders of the company and got them to give him an option on their stock, with the objective of tying up as much as he could. As it turned out, he got options on 51 percent of the stock, effectively blocking Barrett. I was impressed that our quiet and clever founder had headed off the threats of Barrett.

But our founder ran into a problem, and this is where it gets a little tricky. Troy was still on the board of directors, and I suspect he was advised by counsel that, as a fiduciary of the company, he might have a duty not to frustrate Barrett's effort to find the fair market value (FMV) of the stock, because that offer might be more than its then–trading value and in the best interest of the stockholders. So, in a continued effort to get around this new kink in the works, Troy cleverly assigned his options on the Sonic stock to management for an exercise price equal to the FMV. It was an effective assignment, and it took the fiduciary monkey off of the founder's back while keeping Barrett blocked from buying a majority of the outstanding shares and gaining control of the company.

Troy told me years later that the last thing he expected management to do was to exercise that option.

But my boss, the CEO, had secretly been wanting to buy Sonic for quite some time, as I mentioned earlier, and there it was, the opportunity suddenly in our laps. The only thing keeping the CEO and our management team from buying the company was that we had next to no money. So, the only way to get a few million bucks was to seek financing from a bank or some other financial institution and borrow against the company's assets—a leveraged buyout, or LBO. We were all on board, everyone on the management team, so we began the process of seeking out funding so that we could purchase Sonic.

Twelve months and twenty institutions later, we had nothing other than twenty rejections and a nonrefundable $100,000 deposit we had given the company—and we had borrowed 100 percent of that. It was the mid-eighties, a bad time to be talking to anyone in the southwest United States about raising money—the banks were all just about broke by then—and if you were an underfunded, underleveraged group trying to buy a company that didn't have stellar numbers, you might as well have gone to your grandma for the money. The funding we sought was very unlikely. Then, one day, Tom Van Dyke called me.

Tom was a Kansas City corporate and securities lawyer and a member of our company's Board of Directors. He had led our board through an excellent process during this time period to ensure the fiduciary protection of the board and our management team in the situation that was tricky for all of us. I had come to admire Tom, although my boss, the CEO, often grew frustrated with him. My view of this was then and is now that my boss had no background with sticky board governance issues requiring Tom's kind of expertise.

Tom had just closed a deal for another client who was also buying a restaurant chain. The transaction had been financed by Heller Financial, a group with which I was not familiar, but also that had not rejected us. Tom made the point that, were they to do the lending, that would be very expensive, but they were not a commercial bank and operated under different oversight and operating parameters. Tom gave me the name and contact information for Allen Ronin, an officer of Heller. I didn't fully appreciate it yet, but we were off to the races.

We reached out to him based solely on Tom's recommendation. He said they'd take a look at our situation, that he was traveling east to west at the time, and that he could come through town to check us out. It would prove to be one more strange business dealing.

First of all, when Allen came to visit, our CEO wasn't in town. Odd thing number one. So, our treasurer tried to work with him and ended up handing him off to me for a time; he spent most of his day hanging out with me, and I was only legal counsel. That was strange thing number two. Coincidentally, though, I had been reading an article in the business section of the Sunday *New York Times* about John Reed, the then-CEO of Citibank—well, Allen had worked for Citibank and he was a big fan of Reed. Strange thing number three. The two of us sat there for most of the afternoon talking about John Reed and Citibank and what it takes to invest and succeed, and before I knew it, the visit had come to an end. He packed up, left our office, and went back to Los Angeles.

I figured there was no way he had obtained the required information or much else that he wanted, although he had sounded strangely optimistic on his way out the door. Little did I know, he was ready to commit his company to moving forward, and within a matter of days, he sent us a commitment letter for a loan of almost 70 percent of the purchase price. No further due diligence. No meeting with the CEO or our investment banker. None of that. Simply a commitment letter saying, in effect, Heller would finance management's purchase of two-thirds of the purchase price of Sonic, leaving us to still raise the other third. It was a stunning development.

And then in a final, bizarre twist, the VP who made the commitment on behalf of Heller, Allen Ronin, departed Heller in short order. I don't remember the time frame exactly, but I'm pretty sure he quit within a few weeks of sending us the offer letter, so of course at that point we were all sitting around wondering if our dream would follow him out the door. It seemed reasonable to me that Heller would look at the deal, chuckle quietly to themselves, and politely decline. But they didn't.

So there we were, on our way to purchasing Sonic less than a year after Barrett's buyout claim in the CEO's office, the one that started it all and convinced Troy Smith to give the management team an option on 51 percent of the company's outstanding shares. Our investment banker helped us find an investment group in Houston that loaned another 17 percent of the purchase price, subordinated to Heller, then the same firm, along with management, put up cash for ownership of 100 percent of the Sonic equity.

The day came when it was time to make everything official, the day to close this transaction that was ultimately a cash merger, and it was kind of a tough day, because all of the shareholders had to sell, but none of them liked the idea. I remember the day of the closing, people showed up and were extremely unhappy about how things had gone down. I remember even seeing Jim Barrett, the man whose buyout threat had brought this all about. Everyone showed up to the old corporate headquarters, and the deal was finalized and closed.

Personally, at the time, I wasn't even that enthusiastic about the idea of owning shares in Sonic. I didn't see myself staying long-term, and the company wasn't looking particularly strong. Besides, there were things about the transaction that I didn't like very much. I decided at that point that I would put as little into the company as I could and still keep my job. It had been decided that 1 percent of the company would cost $25,000, and that would be the minimum you could purchase, so that's the amount I went for: I borrowed $15,000, rolled in stock options worth around $7,500, and put in $2,500 cash.

That was my contribution to the $10 million purchase of Sonic, and I sat on that minuscule original investment for two and a half years without ever reconsidering my position through selling or doubling down.

Fast forward to December 1988, and we had the opportunity to completely recapitalize our company and buy out the Houston partner who owned 40 percent of the equity of the company. The value of Sonic had risen quite a bit, so by restructuring the ownership, we were able to buy out even more insiders who had left the company. In fact, with this transaction, I would go from owning 1 percent of the company to owning around 8 percent, putting in nothing out of pocket. Because the company had grown so much in value, I was in fact selling my original stake to our newly formed entity at a radical gain, so for my original cash contribution of $2,500, I was able to roll into the new entity, receive 8 percent of the equity (instead of 1 percent before), and receive a payback at closing of $600,000 cash, along with a promissory note for $250,000.

What an extraordinary return in less than three years!

To give you the bigger picture, we bought the company in 1986 at a value of $10 million, recapitalized in 1988 with a value of $35 million, and took it public in 1991 when it was valued at $100 million. By 1991, the 8 percent I had acquired in 1988 was worth $6 million. Mind you, that wasn't the end of it by a long shot—the stock would more than double in the next eight months, taking the value of my Sonic holdings to $15 million.

Talk about opportunity biting you in the butt.

• • •

THERE'S A DIFFERENCE between recognizing an opportunity and being an opportunist. That word—opportunist—is enough to make me cringe. It conjures up all kinds of negative connotations like exploitation, calculation, and profiteering. Do you know someone like that? Someone who exploits circumstances to gain advantage over others? History is full of them.

People like Rasputin. Grigory Yefimovich Rasputin was born in the late 1800s and, after undergoing some form of religious conversion in his youth, traveled from his homeland of western Siberia to Mount Athos in Greece as well as Jerusalem. He began styling himself as a "starets," or self-proclaimed holy man.

When he was in his thirties, he drifted to St. Petersburg, the capital of imperial Russia, and began to acquire a reputation as a mystic who possessed special healing powers. His wild appearance and staring eyes did little to quash the hearsay. He was introduced to Tsar Nicholas II and his wife, Alexandra, whose young son suffered from hemophilia and frequently experienced bouts of uncontrolled bleeding. Nicholas and Alexandra asked for Rasputin's help, and he was able to calm the child and ease his condition, though there's no definitive explanation of how he did so (the top theory is that he used hypnosis[19]). Regardless, from that point on, Rasputin had endless gratitude from the royal family and unfettered access to the royal household.

After the First World War broke out in 1914, Nicholas left to take personal command of Russia's frontline troops, leaving Alexandra in charge of internal affairs. Rasputin, already a court fixture, worked diligently to expand his influence. Together, he and Alexandra were responsible for a string of bad decisions, including the appointment of unqualified favorites to key government posts.

Rasputin used his status and power to full effect and became a controversial figure; he accepted bribes and sexual favors from admirers, was accused by his enemies of religious heresy and rape, was suspected of exerting undue political influence over the tsar, and was even rumored to be having an affair with Alexandra.[20]

To the Russian people, Rasputin symbolized everything that was wrong with imperial government. The court and the royal family became objects of ridicule, to be despised. Rasputin's murder by royalists at the end of 1916 came too late to undo all the damage he had caused, not least of which was driving a wedge between Nicholas and his people. Shortly after Rasputin's death, revolution broke out and Nicholas was forced to abdicate his throne.

The fall of the three-century-old Romanov dynasty may be an extreme example of what can happen when someone manipulates an opportunity for selfish gain, but it's a true representation of the lengths some people will go to script their success. Alternatively, many people wander and assemble success as they go, stumbling upon opportunities and optimizing them with a pure intention and wild curiosity. There's a whole spectrum in between, of course, with varying degrees of hard work, purposeful planning, and spontaneous pursuits.

• • •

SO WHAT BECAME of the Wile E. Coyote Jim Barrett? He attempted to create an opportunity for himself with no invitation to include others. This is not the kind of opportunity I am suggesting is one to seize; my position is to share the obligations, but share the wealth too!

When Barrett approached us about buying the company and firing us, he owned about thirty Sonic Drive-Ins. Two of his peers had similarly sized operations: Darrell Rogers and Bobby Merritt. After the management bought the company in 1986, Barrett approached management in 1987 about paying a flat amount to our company as his franchisor and then departing the Sonic system, taking his stores with him. Management was very agreeable to doing so.

Fast-forward thirty years to my retirement from Sonic. Jim Barrett's operations had not grown appreciably in store count; they may have grown in sales, but we were never able to confirm that. The respective businesses of his contemporaries Darrell Rogers and Bobby Merritt, whose businesses were on par with Barrett's in 1987, had exploded in scale as Sonic exploded. Their store counts had grown ten times over, their revenues twenty times over, and their personal wealth exceptional by any standard.

Barrett had caused an opportunity to arise that came to change my life and the business careers of many others. In his obituary in 2016, however, I recall almost no mention of his business career.

RULE OF THUMB #5:
Seize Opportunity Created by Others.

What if it's not all about you? Leaning on only one's own ability to create opportunities is a tough, often long road, with a higher rate of failure than success. That's why we have to learn to see and seize opportunities that others created. These opportunities are everywhere for the taking, but you have to be able to see them; you have to be able to see the whole picture at the same time. I like to call it "circular vision." That is, seeing the whole picture all the time—for both what it is and what it could be. It's less about using your rational, strategic mind than invoking your intuition and inquisitiveness—and then being prepared for anything. If you're focused on only those opportunities you can originate, you'll likely miss more opportunities than you realize, and perhaps even the best opportunities before you.

Do you notice the things around you? Historically those who embrace this eyes-wide-open approach—no matter if it's second nature or a conscious effort—tend to make momentous, life-changing discoveries. Most of them didn't do it alone either—meaning, they weren't the first to stumble upon the opportunity, but were the first to actualize it by leveraging their circumstances.

Christopher Columbus is renowned for discovering the Americas, but he didn't create boats or maps or maritime exploration. In fact, he wasn't even the first European to have set foot on continental North America—that was a Norse explorer from Iceland named Leif Ericsson centuries before. But it was Columbus's voyages and efforts that brought the Americas to the attention of Europe and initiated the enduring association between the two. Explains historian Martin Dugard: "Columbus's claim to fame isn't that he got there first, it's that he stayed."

Patsy Sherman didn't invent fluorochemical rubber, but when it spilled onto a coworker's tennis shoe, she saw more than a stubborn material that couldn't be removed. She saw Scotchgard, a spill to protect against all spills.

Craig Newmark sent an email to ten friends to discuss upcoming social events in the San Francisco area. When other people began emailing him asking if they could be added to the cc list, he noticed that their interests expanded to jobs or something for sale. In 1997, he launched Craigslist.org.

Noah McVicker created a substance for his family's soap company as a wallpaper cleaner. It wasn't a huge success. Noah's nephew, Joseph McVicker, saw that the putty-like substance didn't contain any toxic chemicals and could be reused. He thought it would be a good modeling compound to make art and craft projects at school and Play-Doh was born.

It is my belief that it's either arrogant or strategically lazy to think success and enjoyment will come quickest by "making your own way." We don't have to do that, because the opportunities others have created all around us are usually more evolved and more efficient. So the key is not to be an opportunity creator as much as it is to be an opportunity spotter. I'm not saying we should be unoriginal thieves. I'm saying that opportunities aren't owned, so seizing one that someone else created isn't stealing—it's noticing something no one conceived of before.

Life

When's the last time you had a fruitful conversation? One that filled you up and left you feeling enlightened and hopeful? The exchanging of thoughts, feelings, ideas, or information is a daily occurrence that, in my opinion, isn't properly appreciated for all it can mean to our current trajectories. A simple conversation can prompt a ripple effect that opens the door to an unforeseen opportunity.

We've all heard the saying that it's not what you know, it's who you know. In the world of networking in which we now live, you never know when talking with someone will turn out to be the *right* someone—the someone with a connection or an "in" that leads to a lucky break. It's happened to me countless times. I've offhandedly mentioned something and the person with whom I was speaking had an unexpected insight, tip, introduction, or perspective to offer. The conversation in and of itself was a seized opportunity, but then served as a catalyst for bigger and better opportunities.

Everyone you will ever meet knows something you don't.

What can you learn from them? What can you see? What opportunity can arise from your exchange? Conversations allow us to sow seeds wherever we go—in people, in jobs, in new ventures and experiences—and we never know for certain which seeds will sprout, but we trust the more we sow, the greater the potential harvest.

Work

The amount of things that can go wrong at work are endless. I'm willing to bet that just reading that sentence conjured up a certain memory of when something specific went awry on your watch. Maybe you didn't hit your sales goal, quota, or deadline. Maybe you were unprepared for a meeting or missed it altogether. Maybe you let a team member down or vice versa. Maybe your big pitch crashed and burned. It happens to the best of us because failure is inevitable, as much in our professional life as in our personal one.

The good news is that opportunity can be found in failure. All of business is an experiment, and as is the essence of experiments, we won't know until we try. Failure tells us what doesn't work so we can pivot and find what does work, faster; it's an opportunity to reconfigure our approach. Thomas Edison constructed thousands of different theories in connection with the theory of the light bulb before it was successful. "I have not failed. I've just found 10,000 ways that won't work," he said.

Opportunities are everywhere and they're ours for the taking, and sometimes failing is the surest way to propel us toward them. What opportunities can you find through failing? How can you use what broke down to build it back up differently?

Leadership

There are many attributes that go into being a successful leader. Ask a dozen experts, and you'd likely get a dozen answers, among them things like commitment, agility, strategy, discipline, accountability, or humility. What you may not hear—although I hope you would—is listening. Having effective listening skills is essential when it comes to successful leadership and can be the key to identifying opportunities that wouldn't have come to light otherwise.

When was the last time you were a sounding board for someone and it led to their aha! moment? What positive results have come from actively listening to your team and their thoughts? Instead of immediately jumping in to give advice or trying to troubleshoot a problem, a good rule is to ask open-ended questions. Curiosity can go a long way, and it starts by shifting the focus to being interested rather than being interesting. Eventually, you'll ask a question no one else has asked before. The answer can be what inspires productive change and meaningful opportunities for those you lead. After all, the intention here is not to find opportunities for you or your business; it's to find opportunities for *them*, the people who look to you as their leader. If those opportunities are business related, it may come back to benefit you anyway, but that needs to be the side effect and not the objective.

What will you hear if you focus less on what you have to say and more on what the people around you are saying? What will come from it? What opportunities will sprout, grow, and become something all their own?

CHAPTER 6

Innovation Is Not a Luxury

When I took over as CEO in April 1995, Sonic was a fairly strong company, fundamentally speaking. We had gone public in 1991 at $12.50 a share, and I became CEO in 1995 at $25 a share. While that sounds really strong, doubling in four years, we had in fact hit $32 a share in January of 1992. So, in reality, the stock had been stagnating for around three years when I took the helm. Our profits per share had grown nicely throughout this time, but our rate of growth was slowing each year and we were operating below market expectations.

More succinctly, while our earnings grew every year, our rate of growth was contracting so our price-earnings ratio (the multiple of earnings the market pays for growth) was also contracting. In a three-year period, our absolute earnings per share had doubled twice, but the price of our stock had declined.

We had plans underway to grow the business, but the main initiatives I wanted to see get some traction at that point had a very long arc to them. They weren't things that would bring a return in one or two quarters—they were objectives that would need buy-in at all levels, from store managers to franchisees to corporate employees and even the board. They were objectives like store-level retrofits, new store construction, and development of new products, all of which would take time and none of which were quick fixes. If I was going to make it for the long haul, our team needed to build consensus. And I needed to be flexible, open to innovations I could not possibly have foreseen or imagined.

As I eased into my first months and years at Sonic, I realized how important innovation would be to my success, to our success. In a business the size of Sonic, innovation isn't some kind of luxury, something you have as a cute tagline or bullet point. Innovation, and diversity of business, must become a way of life. It has to become the expectation, the norm. You have to be looking for it all the time, because if you're not ready, if you're not continuously in search of innovation, it may surface for a moment, but it will appear in your competitors' businesses!

• • •

I REMEMBER WHEN I was first approached by one particular franchisee. He explained that there were some officers in the company on his back. They wanted him to change the direction of his store because it didn't fall within the accepted norms of a Sonic location.

One of the main challenges of operating a franchise business is trying to discern when a franchisee's innovations would make brilliant additions to the franchise community and when a franchisee's innovations need to be nipped in the bud. Franchisees are businesspeople, and they are always coming up with new ideas—some of these ideas will work well on a large scale, while others, if only done at a handful of stores, threaten to dilute the brand. If enough franchisees are doing their own thing, you run the risk of a franchise losing its identity.

I hadn't heard of any conflict with this particular franchisee. He was a strong operator.

"What are you doing that's so threatening to our brand?" I asked him, smiling.

"It's my ice-cream program," he said.

You should know that this franchisee was well known and respected in our system. He was forty years old, but he had been in Sonic for probably twenty-five years, his father having owned and operated Sonic franchises when he was a teenager. His dad had died young, and he had inherited the business. Because he ran strong locations and normally worked within our system, I was interested to hear his story.

"I haven't heard anything about your ice-cream program," I said, my interest rising. "What's going on?"

"Your guys are telling me they don't like it because it makes my stores too much like Dairy Queen. And we're not Dairy Queen."

"Well, that's true, we're not Dairy Queen. What are you doing?"

I was really working to understand his dilemma. Listening, as a business application, will change the course of your business, change the course of your career, in many incredible ways. If you want to spot possible innovations, you have to be a good listener.

"Here in Oklahoma and Texas," he said, "the stores we have, we don't do all that much in ice-cream sales. But in the Carolinas, ice cream makes all the difference in the world."

"Well, what's your number-one store? What percentage of your sales at that store is ice cream?"

He looked at me for a moment before going on. I'll tell you right now—I knew the numbers on our systemwide ice-cream sales, and our average store did between 3 and 5 percent. It was a nice little program, a good add-on, but relatively insignificant when compared to the burgers and fries we were selling. At that time, our average unit volume, or AUV, was around $600,000, so our average drive-in probably had ice-cream sales around $25,000 per annum.

"My number-one store?" he said.

"Yeah."

"In my number-one store, ice-cream sales are about thirty percent."

Well, I almost fell over. I couldn't believe it. This guy's

top store was approaching $200,000 in ice-cream sales. I immediately knew we were talking big numbers if applied on a systemwide basis. This could have some huge potential.

"That's extraordinary," I said when I rediscovered my voice. "Can you tell me what you're doing? Why are you selling so much ice cream?"

He went on to describe in detail this comprehensive program that they ran. They didn't just sell shakes and one kind of a cone and maybe an ice-cream sundae. They had a broader program that included a banana split, plus local promotions that brought people to the store on different days. They were having huge success. When he finished describing what they were doing, I was incredibly impressed.

"Look," I said, "I'm sending someone to come look at your program. Don't change anything yet." It had occurred to me that every store in our system had a soft-serve ice-cream machine, but most of the system had no program and, collectively, we were not promoting this product. The upside was huge.

That was the summer of 1994. By 1995, we were testing a program, borrowing his idea and refining it. We tested it in two different markets—Lafayette, Louisiana, and Houston, Texas. And even though it was wintertime, the tests were hugely successful. By 1996, we had this Frozen and Fountain Favorites program rolling through our entire system, and we backed it up with an advertising push in May.

At that time, a good number for growth of same-store sales might have been 4–5 percent. In the first full month of the new ice-cream program, May 1996, our systemwide sales increased 12 percent. The following summer was our strongest summer in years.

In fiscal year 1997, the first full fiscal year in which we had our Frozen and Fountain Favorites, store-level profits leaped almost 40 percent.

It's not an overstatement to say that ice cream transformed our business. Franchisees' personal incomes exploded, which meant they wanted additional stores, so new store build-outs took off. Soon we were retrofitting old units to incorporate the new brand, and our marketing budget went through the roof.

From 1997 to 2001, our systemwide sales (the sum of all drive-in sales, company-owned and franchised combined) went from $1 billion to $2 billion.

By 2001, we had split our stock three times in my tenure, with a 3-for-2 split each time. The value of our company had more than doubled. In my first five years as CEO, we produced more incremental annual system sales growth than the highest annual system sales the brand had produced in the preceding forty years.

The point of the story is, it would have been easy for me, as a franchisor, to look at that innovative franchisee and say, "I'm sorry, but you need to get your operations back in line with our expectations." And I could have probably done it in a palatable way, maintaining our relationship with that franchisee. And we would have gone on as if nothing had happened.

Instead, his innovation became our innovation. And this one innovation, funding many others in turn, transformed our company and our brand. More subtly, however, it gave our customers a different reason to visit our stores. Historically, most of our sales occurred at lunch and dinner. With the roll-out of drinks and ice cream, our afternoon and evening traffic exploded. This lesson gave us different things to think about prospectively, like what other parts of our customer's day (breakfast, for instance) we could serve and what other ways we could engage customers (like credit cards and, later, ordering and payment apps). This one insight was a gift that kept giving.

• • •

INNOVATION IS EVERYTHING. If you're not willing to open up your eyes and see unexpected possibilities, then business of the future is the wrong business for you. Focusing your attention or your business or your life on one thing, without taking off the blinders every so often, will most likely lead you to run yourself into the ground. Look around. There is a world of possibilities, of new paths, just waiting for you.

Consider the case of Harriet Williams Russell, born in Buffalo, New York, in 1844. After marrying Charles Strong at the age of nineteen, she moved to the San Gabriel Valley in California, where they built a home on a ranch and had four daughters. While Charles initially made a fortune in banking, publishing, and mining, he ultimately proved to be an unsavvy businessman and they fell into extreme debt. Depressed and disappointed, Charles took his own life and left Harriet alone to handle the ranch, the children, and, yes, the debt.

One day while walking her land in search of a stable crop, Harriet came upon a grove of walnut trees. Walnuts require constant moisture, but the water supply at the ranch was less than ideal. So what did Harriet do? She set out to find a way to ensure more water and realized she could provide a consistent flow if she optimized rainfall. So she designed an irrigation system and began yielding profitable returns—eventually becoming the leading commercial grower of walnuts in the country. But why stop there?

She went on to drill a number of artesian wells on her estate and, to utilize the water she obtained, installed a pumping plant. She then incorporated her property as an official water company, of which she became president. But why stop there?

She studied water problems, including the control of flood waters and water storage, and advocated for water conservation and new approaches to arid land agriculture. She was granted a patent for a dam and reservoir construction, and went before Congress to present a plan she had designed to dam the Colorado River. She obtained another patent on a new method for impounding debris and storing water, for which she was awarded two medals by the World's Columbian Exposition.[21] But she didn't stop there.

Following her ingenuity and passion for inventing, Harriet Williams Russell Strong went on to patent three more inventions: a device for raising and lowering windows, a hook and eye, and a window sash holder.[22] She also found she had considerable talent as a musical composer and published a number of songs and a book of musical sketches. She became the vice president of the Los Angeles Symphony Orchestra Association, as well as the first female member of the Los Angeles Chamber of Commerce.

Harriet could have very well kept her head down and focused on saving her fledgling ranch based on the way it had always been run, but can you imagine if she had? She chose to consider the possibilities, and soon found herself on the cusp of something new, something really exciting, that would quite literally alter the world. Innovation and its benefits don't come to those who are narrowly focused. Innovation comes to those who are willing to try something new, sometimes just for the hell of it.

Another example is Reed Hastings.

Born in Boston in 1960, Hastings studied mathematics at Bowdoin College, served in the U.S. Marine Corps, and traveled two years with the Peace Corps, most of which was spent in Swaziland teaching math. When he came back to the United States (with all of that incredible experience under his belt), he returned to school, earning a master's degree in computer science from Stanford. After that he became a software developer, founded Pure Atria Corporation, and sold it in 1997 for a lot of money.

Hastings was now in his late thirties, well-off, and free

to do whatever he wanted. I don't know what most people do when they become independently wealthy in their thirties, but Hastings wasn't one to just sit around, enjoying his newfound wealth. Instead, he partnered up with Marc Randolph and created a subscription-based movie-rental service we now know as Netflix.

In those early years, the Netflix model was pretty simple: customers could rent an unlimited number of DVDs for a set fee, up to three at one time, and everything was sent and returned through the old-fashioned mail service. Once a customer finished with one DVD and sent it back, the next one on their list shipped out automatically. Simple and brilliant, and since DVDs were just gaining traction at the time, it was an idea at the forefront of technology.

Their innovation to that time was exceptional, so imagine my surprise when a former Blockbuster executive years later told me that his team had declined the opportunity to buy Netflix for $100 million. They liked the Blockbuster model better—perhaps you don't remember Blockbuster, except as a cautionary tale of how *not* to innovate.

Either way, Netflix grew as executives managed to create movie studio partnerships, carry an impressive line of indie films, and market aggressively. In February of 2007, Netflix reached an incredible mile marker: they shipped their one billionth DVD. And soon after that, they were developing one of the first movie-streaming websites in the industry.[23]

Aside from one pricing misstep, Netflix has somehow managed to stay ahead of the curve in an industry that seems to transform on a continual basis. That's the challenge you face as a business leader. In an ever-changing world, how will you transition from what works today to what is going to work tomorrow? When someone in your company tries to turn things on its head (by introducing ice cream, for example), what will your response be? Ridicule? Shut them down? Feel threatened somehow? Put them off? Or will you listen, look for advantages, and encourage the kind of innovation that might just save your company?

Hastings and his crew could have tied themselves to the DVD snail-mail model. They could have seen the streaming thing coming but thought it required too much work or too much learning or too much money. They could have decided to double down on their DVD mailing business. And if they had, Netflix would probably still be limping along, trying to wring as much profit out of a shrinking group of people in the world, people who still only watch movies on DVDs. And in another twenty years? They would be the next Blockbuster, a business that people remembered fondly but no longer used.

But they didn't sit on their existing success. Hastings and his team continued to innovate, continued looking for new ways to deliver the very thing their customers were coming to them for: entertainment. This is the key—they realized they weren't a DVD business, they were an entertainment business. And it's this dedication to innovation that has brought Netflix to the place where they have over 100 million worldwide subscribers.

Netflix has embraced innovation in the technology they use to help subscribers find the right movie and then make sure the viewing of it goes well. Netflix uses something called deep learning to predict and suggest what movies you might like to watch next, making their service even more useful to users. Netflix has also used state-of-the-art technology to ensure the movies are delivered in a format that is smooth, watchable, and high-quality. They even have technology that helps people on slow internet connections watch action flicks without seeing the dreaded buffering symbol.

But beyond the technology, Hastings proved his genius for innovation when he shifted the company's focus to developing original content. In fact, in October 2017, Netflix announced plans to spend $8 billion toward its goal of having at least half of the content on its site be content original to Netflix. They have transitioned from being a shipping company to a production company. They have gone from storing and mailing DVDs to creating and producing brand-new movies and shows, with innovative creations like *Stranger Things*, *Orange Is the New Black*, and *Narcos* taking the entertainment world by storm. They've earned nine Primetime Emmy Awards and four Golden Globe Awards, plus a growing list of Oscar nominations.[24]

One important thing to remember about innovating, and one reason so many people and businesses never commit to it, is that you never arrive. There's never a point where you can sit back and say, *Ah, here we are, now we are finished.*

There's always something new to try, something fresh to implement. This can, at times, be exhausting. Let's just admit that we all crave, from time to time, a moment to relax, to sit back, to catch our breath. At Sonic, we went on from ice cream and tried many different things in the following years. You can see this with Hastings at Netflix too. One innovation leads to another, which leads to another. If you're good, or lucky, innovation will lead to one win after another.

Netflix understands that they're not an isolated company working in a vacuum—they have competition. And that's important to keep in mind: when should you watch your competitors and try to keep up, and when are you going to forget about them and forge ahead? In a 2017 investor report, Netflix claimed they are not trying to copy Amazon because they believe there is enough time in the world for people to watch both Netflix and Amazon Prime (Amazon's streaming service). But Netflix does have its eyes on YouTube.

"We've definitely got YouTube envy," says Netflix CEO Hastings. "I remember that YouTube announced they were 1 billion [hours of video] a day, and when we looked it up, we're a little over 1 billion a week. So, we've got a long way to go to catch up . . ."[25]

This is another important part of maintaining an environment and a culture of innovation: having goals out there that you are aggressively pursuing. Have someone you're chasing. One billion hours of video-watching a day is Netflix's crazy goal.

What's yours?

Remember, though, that pleasure is the child of pain. Successful innovation always requires a lot of work, some painful decisions, and breaking away from things you thought were crucial or important. The benefits of innovation are rarely reaped at the outset, and the sacrifices you make always imply a kind of delayed gratification and patience, which yields a greater appreciation of the benefits when they finally occur.

From 1994 to 2000, we at Sonic undertook a multiyear series of major initiatives that included license renegotiations, branding efforts, new menus, new products, new employee uniforms, new television creative, new promotions, and a multiyear explosion of store-level sales. Those years represented some intense work, some difficult conversations, and some serious growing pains that a lot of businesses find difficult to negotiate or even survive. But all of that hard work paid off. It had taken us forty-four years to reach $1 billion in sales, but only four years, from 1997 to 2001, to reach $2 billion. And that sales surge came about because of the innovation at virtually all levels of our business—even in the way we explained our growth strategy to investors, which was no small feat. The man behind that was Scott McLain. Scott came to our company as vice president and treasurer around 1995. About two years later, he became chief financial officer and, later still, president of our franchising company, Sonic Industries. In addition to having very strong selling instincts, Scott was bright and creative, and understood how we made money and even more how to explain that to the stock market. It was Scott who developed the term "multi-layered growth strategy" to synthesize into a single concept the contribution to earnings of our:

1. Same-store sale growth, plus
2. Ascending royalty rate, plus
3. New franchise store openings, plus
4. Company-owned, new-store growth, plus
5. Profit margin expansion of company stores, plus
6. Stock repurchase contributions to EPS growth.

He effectively showed our investors how a 2–3 percent kick to #1 could yield a 16–18 percent growth to #6. His ability to innovatively articulate the quality of our growth story to the market was no small factor in our achieving six 3-for-2 stock splits from 1996 through 2006.

RULE OF THUMB #6:
Focus Is Necessary but Not Sufficient for Innovation.

Great innovators never look at their current realities—they look ahead. The Wright brothers saw a bird flying freely through the air and wondered why people couldn't do the same thing. Thomas Edison wanted people to be able to see the world at night. Walt Disney noted parents' boredom after he accompanied his daughters to a filthy and unfriendly amusement park and felt there should be "some kind of family park where parents and children could have fun together." They were seemingly out-of-the-blue ideas followed by years of nose-to-the-grindstone work.

We admire people whose creative genius arrives in sudden sparks of inspiration, but we also revere people who work incredibly long and hard for their breakthroughs. Most people are either one or the other: the ideating visionary with their head in the clouds or the hyperfocused worker who carries out the vision. But does it have to be a dichotomy? Dreamers versus doers, creativity versus discipline, right brain versus left brain? The examples above were people who encapsulated both sides of the coin, which is uncommon but not impossible.

In his breakthrough book, *The Spark and the Grind*, artist Erik Wahl discusses this very thing—namely, how the most potent individual creators in any environment or industry have learned how to be both. One of many examples Wahl discusses is Isaac Newton. His first spark came in the form of the idea for the windmill, of which he went on to build a working model at age eleven. In his mid-twenties, he discovered the color spectrum and calculus, and in his mid-forties, he discovered and published his findings on the three laws of motion. He became a renowned innovator because he repeatedly stoked the sparks of his imagination and then paired it with curiosity and hard work.

Being diligent is not enough, nor is having great ideas; being an ignitor does us no good if we can't keep the fire going. Take Martin Luther King Jr. He had a dream and stoked it into a blaze that transformed our nation. Would the spark have ignited as it did if King had only given a single speech?

To stay at the forefront of innovation, we need to strike a balance between the discipline of thinking and the discipline of doing. We must keep our eyes wide open to avoid narrowly focusing on one path, one solution, or one side of our brain. We must make a commitment to look around and ahead as much as we look down and through. We need to chase the spark and embrace the grind, not at the expense of each other but in conjunction with one another.

Life

Life is full of ruts—we get stuck in old habits, familiar patterns, and daily routines, and stay there for a number of reasons. Maybe it's because we seek comfort or convenience. Maybe we're methodical and prefer sameness. Maybe we feel that our ruts have served us well and we're of the mindset that if it ain't broke, don't fix it. Regardless, we must ask ourselves if we've stayed in those ruts because we truly believe we've hit our groove or stride, or because we're stuck.

Take a look at where you are today and where you'd like to be in the future. Have you plateaued on the way up the corporate ladder, on the way down the scale, on the way forward in your love life? Consider your day-to-day habits, patterns, and routines. Are they propelling you toward what you want or prohibiting you from attaining your goals and aspirations? Is complacency keeping you from innovating something important?

Our habits, patterns, and routines can often keep us from reaching our full potential, although the exact opposite can also be true: our habits, patterns, and routines can be what helps us reach our potential. It doesn't have to be one or the other. We need discipline as much as we need disruption; consistency as much as adaptation; imagination as much as focus. For you to ensure dynamic growth in your personal life, what should stay the same and what can be tweaked in order to maximize your effectiveness?

Work

Would you rather fill in Excel sheets with data for eight hours or come up with new and exciting ideas? I assume you'd opt for the latter. The opportunity to innovate is something most of us want more of in our daily lives, yet often, we feel we can't be more creative at work because of factors beyond our control. Maybe your company is risk-averse, or your targets are intimidatingly aggressive, or the sheer size of your to-do list makes adding anything new feel impossible. Innovation can be likened to a muscle group: the more you actively use it, the stronger, better, and more unstoppable it becomes. What can you do on the job to flex your innovation muscles, so to speak?

We all have parts of our job we feel we can do with our

eyes closed—it's part of what makes us excel in our role but also part of what blinds us to opportunities. What are the daily tasks that you perform without thinking? How can you go about them differently? Finding a new way of doing the same old thing could provide a small yet significant shift in perspective.

If you're feeling underwhelmed at work, you're likely not the only one. Think about picking a colleague you feel comfortable with and making yourself accountable to each other to try new things: go to a new place for lunch, pitch an idea in an unorthodox manner, or just do some old-fashioned brainstorming. Innovation rarely happens in a vacuum, and having an encouraging friend may make incremental change seem that much more substantial.

Leadership

Some of the best innovators in history owe their success to collaboration. Where would Steve Jobs be without Steve Wozniak? What about Bill Hewlett without Dave Packard? William Procter without James Gamble? Paul McCartney without John Lennon? The mere act of working together wasn't what led to their success; it was the individual strengths that each brought to the table. They were what the other wasn't; they had what the other didn't.

It's a good lesson in balance. If you're set in your ways on one end of the spectrum, maybe it's time you bring in someone on the other end to balance you out: the right brain to your left brain, the grinder to your ignitor, the yin to your yang. In our efforts to try to be well-rounded leaders—or, at the very least, multifaceted ones—we may not want to admit our own shortcomings and/or see how they can negatively affect our teams.

Now take a look at those you lead. How can you begin to foster a collaborative environment for them? Are there some people who could use a little balance of their own? Some may be coming up short in one area or another, and others may have an abundance to share. Take the time to observe your colleagues' strengths and needs and see how you can help bridge the gaps.

CHAPTER 7

Your "And" Matters More Than Your "What"

I can hear the wheels spinning in your head now, thoughts of innovation and the next new thing. It can mess with you a little bit, when you first start trying to focus on what might be next, because most of the time, well, you don't know what's next. How can you prepare yourself for opportunities of which you are not yet aware? Is it a mindset? Does it involve some kind of regular practice, either mentally, physically, or spiritually, that might keep you in a place where new opportunities do not appear as interruptions?

I think some of the stuff we've already talked about comes into play. First, a curious person should naturally be open to opportunity, within a reasonable spectrum. So if you are cultivating your sense of curiosity, if you are seeking deep answers to the questions that pop up around you, you'll be more open to opportunities as they appear. A naturally curious person is more predisposed to recognize opportunity than someone who is not curious about anything.

And then more questions come up, right? I mean, if you're really going to dig into this concept of being ready to embrace new opportunities, there are a lot of things to consider. Such as, what makes an interruption an opportunity or a hindrance? How do you know that when an idea or a concept or a new way of doing things interrupts your workflow, it's something to embrace and not something to shove out of the way?

It comes back to the issues of strategic focus and team alignment. If, as you reflect on it, an unscheduled or unplanned-for event seems to be helping you to achieve your objectives better than you were doing before the interruption, then it must be an opportunity. But if it doesn't, if the interruption is bogging down your systems and causing havoc, then maybe you need to ask one more question before setting it aside.

That question is this: Will the interruption help you address a higher priority than the priorities of your existing plan? Does this new interruption have even more potential than the thing that got interrupted?

If you respond affirmatively to questions like this, then you might have an opportunity on your hands. If you answer negatively, then it's probably a hindrance.

But the curious mind is always open, either way—always open to questioning and reconsidering your path.

• • •

AROUND 2001, I attended a small executive conference in Chicago sponsored by Visa and one of the industry's leading magazines, *Nation's Restaurant News*. There were some breakout sessions, talks by industry experts, and of course the normal schmoozing that goes on at those kinds of events. As Visa was one of the headline sponsors, I expected to hear quite a bit from them as the conference went on.

During one of the presentations, a Visa representative talked to us about the surveys done on how women shop, what their patterns are, and how to make your business more women-friendly. Specifically, the Visa rep had some compelling stats on sales being linked to how easily usable credit cards are at your business. More narrowly, she said when it comes to food purchasing decisions for the family, women make the choices a majority of the time, children second, and men third. It seems obvious today, but back in 2001, it was news that women are twice as likely to shop at your store if you accept credit cards.

This got me thinking. When I returned to the office, I shared the data and suggested that we consider adding a "pay-at-the-pump" feature at each of our menu-housing units. It would be like a service station where people (women) would feel comfortable pulling up, ordering through the speaker, and then paying with their card, curbside. I was pretty excited about the idea.

Months later, no discernible progress had been made to implement this idea. I looked around the table during one of our senior management team meetings and could not figure out what was holding this initiative back. I realized that one departing senior management member had viewed the program as a hindrance to his staff. An interruption.

In a way, maybe you couldn't blame him. The idea may have seemed to come out of left field. Perhaps I didn't sell the idea sufficiently. Maybe it just didn't rank with his priorities (he was a little hardheaded). Either way, with that senior manager gone and a second moved out of the way, I bore down harder and really pushed it through, and, thanks to Bill Klearman, a technology innovator then a member of our middle management team, the initiative began moving faster. Within months, we had a test in place, and less than a year later we were rolling out PAYS (Pay at Your Stall) across the system.

The impact on sales was immediate and lasting. As we watched the numbers climb, it became clear what an incredible innovation PAYS was. From 2003 through 2018, 100 percent of our system's incremental sales—$2.5 billion—could be attributed to credit card transactions and our customers' use of PAYS.

Just imagine if our unimaginative officer had had his way?

If your organization is not aggressive in the way it says yes to new opportunities, you're not using your resources or your team's energy effectively. You and the people you work with have to be willing to say yes to something even before you know whether or not it will be productive; adopting this attitude will have all kinds of side benefits. It forces you to assume positive intent whenever an idea is brought forward. It causes you to approach any challenge that arises with an open mind on how to respond and what ideas might bring about a positive resolution. When you're more willing to say yes, you become more innovative in your responses and your reactions.

Most important, having this kind of yes mentality will allow you to see things in an "and" context instead of a "but" one. Let me explain.

Your "and" matters more than your "what." Giving yourself permission to take an interest in some things on the side will help you reach your goals, maintain an interest in the important things in your life, and help you become a more well-rounded human being. I know, I know—the advice today is to specialize, spend 10,000 hours doing one thing, become the expert.

But I'm just not sure that's the way that works for most people. If you look back through history, sure, there were plenty of people who focused on one thing, and that became the thing they were known for. But it seems to me there were even more who were successful because they branched out, sought new opportunities, and explored fields completely unrelated to each other.

Take Benjamin Franklin, for example. Born in Boston in what was then known as the Massachusetts Bay Colony, Franklin was his father's fifteenth child and his youngest son.

He thrived at school but was pulled out at ten years of age to help his father's candle and soap shop. When that didn't seem to capture the boy's imagination, Franklin was apprenticed out to a print shop run by one of his older brothers. His brother was rather "harsh and tyrannical," so Benjamin ended up fleeing to New York, and finally Philadelphia, where he would create his legacy—by not becoming an expert in any one thing. In fact, Franklin would become one of the best examples of a Renaissance man you could ever encounter.

He is perhaps best known for his participation in the Second Continental Congress and the part he took in drafting the Declaration of Independence. As one of our nation's Founding Fathers, his influence put him right up there with George Washington.

The accomplishments he was able to see during his lifetime are the envy of any statesman. Start a new nation? Check. Oversee the founding documents for this new country? Check. Negotiate treaties and alliances for this new country? Check. He basically has an unmatched résumé.

And if you go by the current wisdom of focus and expertise, you might conclude that he surely spent the majority of his life and time learning about politics, being an ambassador, and reading the more important political tomes of his time. After all, if he was going to get his 10,000 hours in as an expert politician, how would he have time for anything else?

But if you think Benjamin Franklin spent his entire life completely focused on being a politician, you would be sorely mistaken. His contributions to society, and his interests in general, extended far beyond the world of politics, government, and statehood. And this diversity of interest began at an early age.

When he was still a kid, Franklin became a rather expert swimmer, practicing right there in the Schuylkill River in Philadelphia. On one legendary boating trip in England later in his life, nineteen-year-old Franklin reportedly swam the Thames, all the way from Chelsea to Blackfriars, around 3.5 miles. Not only did he swim it, he performed tricks the entire way, entertaining his fellow travelers, though they were boat-bound. He would even be posthumously inducted into the International Swimming Hall of Fame in 1968.[26] Now there's something you wouldn't expect of a lifelong politician and statesman.

He was also, as we know from the story of the lightning bolt and the kite, obsessed with electricity and even created an entire vocabulary for the field. So few people had experimented with it before that there simply weren't words for many of the things he encountered. One scholar has suggested as many as twenty-five electrical terms, words like battery, brushed, charged, and electrician, were first introduced into the English language by Franklin.[27] Clearly, his knowledge of government didn't hinder his ability to grow in knowledge in, what was at that point, a fledgling field.

And even if Franklin was primarily regarded as a statesman, most of us are aware of at least a few of his many inventions—the more well-known ones being bifocal glasses, the Franklin stove (which heated more efficiently), and the lightning rod. But did you know he also invented the glass harmonica (the "armonica"), a mechanical arm for reaching books on high shelves, the rocking chair, the odometer, and, thank goodness, the flexible urinary catheter?

He also helped establish America's first hospital, founded in Philadelphia in 1751, along with Dr. Thomas Bond. Later in life he recounted: "I do not remember any of my political maneuvers, the success of which gave me at the time more pleasure (than the hospital)." And there was his military career, in which he led troops during the French and Indian War, when things weren't going well for the British and the French (along with their Native allies) since more and more British ground was being taken over by the Americans. He managed to oversee the building of a fort at a Moravian settlement, cleared the area of enemies, and even constructed additional fortresses. But of course, while he was leading the men, he was also creating new and better ways of doing things: he introduced the use of dogs as aids to the guards, began handing out the daily rum ration at the end of the sermon so that more men came to chapel, and even served without pay.[28]

Has there ever been anyone as successful in such disparate fields as Ben Franklin? Inventor, soldier, statesman, electrician, printer . . . swimmer? (To be fair, some other people come to mind. People like Leonardo da Vinci, who was a painter and anatomist; Thomas Jefferson, who was an inventor and politician; Vladimir Nabokov, who was a novelist and entomologist; and Howard Hughes, who was an aviator and filmmaker.)

But what's the point? Is there value in having such wide-ranging interests? Doesn't it make sense to focus on one thing? Wouldn't Ben Franklin have been an even more legendary statesman, perhaps even our country's first president, if he had only focused?

I guess we'll never know the answer to that last question, but I'll tell you this from experience: there are real advantages to including variety in your life, and I think they far outweigh any potential gains you might make from only focusing on one thing. Imagine all of the things Franklin would have had to give up, all the experiences he would have had to forgo, if he had decided at an early age that he was only going to be a newspaper printer, or a politician, or a swimmer, or an electrician. Imagine the things humanity would have missed out on.

There are plenty of good reasons to allow variety to spice up your life.

First of all, when you incorporate Ben Franklin's kind of variety into your life, it increases your natural levels of curiosity. When he started looking into electricity, it opened up his mind to an entirely different field, and it gave him more practice in asking questions. Often, when we focus on only one thing and become better and better at it, even reaching the level of expert, it is easy to become the question answerer and forget how to ask questions. By picking up new interests and entering adjacent fields of study, we are reminded how to stay curious.

Whenever I continue to extend "me," it makes me more creative in all areas. I am sure that Ben Franklin's knowledge of warfare increased his competency as a politician. It's likely that his experiments in electricity contributed to his mechanical skill in printing and made him a better operator of the many presses he owned. And the many hours he spent as a writer surely made him a better statesman. When we add variety to our lives, it stretches us in ways that a singular focus simply cannot.

In 2000, it was brought to my attention that a group in Oklahoma City had come together to work on a public education initiative. Initiatives had passed (referred to as MAPS [Metropolitan Area Projects]) for sports facilities and cultural centers, and the group felt the same should be done for education. Since the court-ordered desegregation efforts of the 1970s, school patrons had defeated a majority of our school bond votes, due in no small part to a 60 percent supermajority approval required under our state constitution. The most recent $50-million bond proposal had "failed" with 58 percent approval.

Consequently, our schools and buses were in bad shape, and technology was antiquated. Accompanying this, the district's student population had a 90 percent poverty level, the district could not balance its books, and finances (bill payment) were not kept current. The district was a mess.

I found myself engaging with a group of a dozen business and political leaders to form a KIDS (Keep Improving District Schools) Committee and conducted a two-year process of school building reviews and community engagement. We then proposed a combination of sales and property taxes totaling $512 million, the renovation of every school and construction of four new schools, the replacement of all school buses, fiber-optic wiring of all schools, new MIS (management information systems) for the HQ building, and a chairmanship of the board for oversight.

Previously, the school board elected a president from its own membership; everyone was in charge, so no one was in charge. As part of this effort, I agreed to stand for the statutorily created chairman position and served as cochair of the campaign with the Oklahoma City mayor.

Our initiatives, dubbed "MAPS for Kids," passed 61 percent to 39 percent after a million-dollar campaign. I ended up serving as board chair from 2001 to 2008, and in that time, as well as soon thereafter, we replaced all school buses, renovated every school, built four new schools, brought all bills current, received a clean district audit for the first time in ten years, and achieved four consecutive years of improvement in average standardized test scores.

This was a punishing task because I was running Sonic at the same time, but it would turn out to be an "and" that meant more to me than I ever expected. I became an advocate, a chairperson, and an activist. It was the public service opportunity of a lifetime, requiring an absolutely unending dedication to improvement.

For many years after, people would stop and thank me for my role in refining the educational landscape in Oklahoma

City. I would always tell them it actually had very little to do with me, it was a team effort, but it meant a great deal to me that they went out of their way to acknowledge the years of hard work. I'd like to believe that what they witnessed may have prompted them to get behind something of their own, something they were passionate about. It's another important benefit of expanding ourselves beyond a laser focus, especially when we work in a business or team environment: expressing our curiosity and creativity might very well encourage those around us to do the same, and even offer inspiration in the projects they're already working on. You really never know who you're inspiring.

After hearing about Franklin's legendary kite experiment where he tied a key to a kite and conducted electricity down from it, a man named Luigi Galvani reportedly began zapping dead frogs with electricity. The electricity, as you might imagine, caused the frogs' legs to jump. This work led Galvani to discover bioelectricity, or the electrical patterns and signals of nerves that trigger processes in muscles and glands. As Galvani continued to pioneer that field of study, his work inspired showmen who set up human corpses attached to electric currents, awakening them. Legend has it that a young woman named Mary Shelley took these experiments and used them as the basis for her world-famous horror story, *Frankenstein*. If all of these legends and tales are true, Benjamin Franklin's influence extended all the way to inspiring the world's first horror novel.

I'll be the first to admit that my interests or discoveries

haven't led to biological developments, book genres, or mass movements, but I do know that they've led to the evolution of who I am as a husband, father, friend, and businessman; they've enhanced my quality of life, added richness to those around me, and had positive effects on my work.

My love of music runs deep, that much you learned a couple chapters back. I'm a self-taught guitarist and piano man, picking up the guitar first in my teens, and later, channeling Billy Joel while sitting down at my family's Baldwin Console. After I started working at Sonic, I learned that several of my coworkers were also music buffs who dabbled as amateur musicians. We started playing together, at first just here and there at one of our homes, and then on a more consistent basis with scheduled rehearsals and consideration of local gigs. We became known as the Sonic Tones, evolving from a casual company band to being asked to perform at the Rock & Roll Hall of Fame. What happened next? Record deals, number-one hits, a world tour? Not a chance. That's never what it was about. It merely gave us joy to stretch our creative muscles and collaborate on something outside of work. It honed our skills and made us better musicians, but more important, it made us better listeners and more empathetic team players.

Though perhaps extraneous examples, adding things like "amateur musician" to my letterhead is fulfilling in an entirely different way than "CEO" or "board member." Exploring those interests has brought me delight and release, allowed me to step back and take a deep breath. When I look at who I am from the nosebleed seats, I see that my adamance in adding variety to my interests has made me a more well-balanced man. I've consciously grown the "ands" and, ultimately, it's taught me that the growth skill that matters most is the discipline to restrain focus and remain versatile.

RULE OF THUMB #7:
Extend Your "Me."

Would you agree that humans love labels? Chief. Lead. Senior. President. Head. One scroll through LinkedIn reveals our commitment to those labels and the esteem we hope stating them will bring us. To some degree it's okay—we've likely earned the designation we've been given, but that doesn't mean it isn't perilous. Assigning labels—or, worse, accepting them—can limit the confines of what we think we can do and what we ascribe for ourselves, which in turn can make life pretty boring.

Our prewiring for predictability explains why we love assigning labels to people and to ourselves. Labeling is simplifying; it's a straightforward way to categorize value. The problem is that humans are not simple, rarely straightforward, and have many redeemable qualities that can't possibly be articulated through a title. One label can never capture all of who we are.

Is your identity wrapped up in a label? What is it? And

I don't just mean a professional one. Titles like mom, dad, coach, caregiver, or volunteer are as honorably earned—more so, in fact—but can feel just as restrictive, as if we finally landed the role we were born to play but are then forever typecast in it. What we're known for—that is, what label we wear—needs to be dynamic and transmutable to reflect the complexity of human experience.

If life is wholly predictable, it will not be enough; there will always be more that we could have done, seen, and become. I'm a firm believer that, deep down, we all long for excitement and adventure. If we live our lives from our head, life becomes predictable, tedious, and safe. But if we live from our hearts, if we access that wanderlust inside us that never quits, then life will be full of curiosity, exploration, and versatility—a life you can't put a label on.

Life

Do you have a bucket list? What kinds of things are on it? Have you crossed any items off yet?

Most of us have a running list of things we want to do, places we want to see, and achievements we want to accomplish before we die. Many times that list is filled with elaborate aspirations like climbing Mount Everest, running a marathon, going skydiving, visiting a far-off country, or writing a book. The sky's the limit, and there's nothing wrong with that—having grand goals gives us something to work toward and keeps us inspired and motivated. But the things we want to accomplish don't always need to be grand; the goals we have for ourselves don't always need to defy odds or break the bank. Think smaller.

What are you curious about? What are you always reading about in magazines? What are you naturally drawn to? Maybe you've always wanted to learn a new language. Maybe you've often thought about taking cooking classes or golf lessons. Maybe you want to involve your spouse, children, or friends in an activity that you can do all together, like joining a book club, buying a plot at a community garden, or going to a rock-climbing gym. Think about what piques your interest that you've yet to pursue. What's stopping you? Pick a simple pleasure, inject it into your life, and see what happens. Do you want to be one of the people who are glad they did? Or one of the people who wish they had?

Work

In this day and age there's a real tendency to be hyper career-focused; our identity is almost inextricably linked to our jobs. Think about the last social gathering you went to—I'm willing to bet one of the first questions that you asked or were asked of you by an unfamiliar face was "What do you do?" There's a temptation to see ourselves as only what it is we do for a living to make money. But we're so much more than that, and if we could allow ourselves to not be so heavily linked to our job title, we would allow ourselves to become more. That doesn't mean you have to always be searching for another job, but it does mean that you can do work—and even sometimes more meaningful work—outside your current job.

There are some pretty famous examples of people whom society knows only for their art and not for what they do behind the scenes. Actor Steven Seagal is a volunteer sheriff deputy and border patrol agent. Los Angeles Angels outfielder Mike Trout is a self-proclaimed "weather geek" who chases storms during the off-season. Singer Tony Bennett is a painter who specializes in landscapes painted with oils and watercolors, and three of his works are even in the Smithsonian. Composer Philip Glass continued to work as a plumber for decades after he found success in the music industry. As the oft-recounted story goes, he was working as a plumber and heard a noise and looked up to find Robert Hughes, the art critic of *Time* magazine, staring at him in disbelief.

"But you're Philip Glass! What are you doing here?" Hughes asked.

To Glass, it was obvious that he was installing Hughes's dishwasher, and he told Hughes he would be finished soon.

"But you are an artist," Hughes protested.

"I am an artist but sometimes I'm a plumber as well, and you should go away and let me finish."

We can lose sight of our purpose so easily in the business

world, getting distracted by deadlines, office politics, and promotions, even if we know full well that that's not what life's about. What can you do outside of work that fulfills something inside you that your profession can't? What's an interest or passion project you can do to fill your cup? As Maya Angelou said: "I've learned that making a living is not the same thing as making a life."

Leadership

Many of the offices within the Sonic headquarters had glass walls, including mine. My office consisted of four glass walls smack dab in the middle of the floor, which, as you can imagine, translated to zero privacy. Granted, people couldn't hear me necessarily, but they could see me at all times.

The glass naturally made me appear more accessible to my coworkers, but that's not why I preferred it. For me, transparent walls acted as a constant reminder that there were other people doing an array of other things, and it helped me value all the other jobs that were getting done. I was never blind to the fact that Sonic's success was in large part thanks to the hardworking individuals whom I observed on a daily basis. The glass also inspired me to get out of my office and learn about the people who surrounded me; it motivated me to want to hear about and stay involved in their lives.

Do you see those you lead? Really *see* them? For who they

are, not just for what they do? Leadership is about people, and you can't lead them unless you value and understand them. If you're talking to a coworker, no matter if it's a janitor or an executive, always remember there's a person behind that job—they're more than a tool or a resource.

CHAPTER 8

Relevance Is a Paradox

Coach Dean Smith led the men's basketball team at the University of North Carolina at Chapel Hill for thirty-six years, and his list of accomplishments could fill this book. Here are some highlights: He retired with 879 career victories, which at the time was the most wins in men's collegiate basketball. He took his team to the Final Four eleven times and won two national championships. He coached the U.S. men's basketball team to Olympic gold in 1976 and was elected to the Basketball Hall of Fame in 1983. He coached arguably the best player to ever play basketball, Michael Jordan, and his innovations are still visible in the game to this day.[29]

Despite his success, despite his inarguable ability to lead, throughout his career he put the team and the players first. In his book *The Carolina Way* (a must-read book for any successful coach), Coach Smith talks about a small travel detail he insisted on whenever the team flew a commercial airline to a game or tournament. The seniors were handed the first-class seats. The tallest remaining players were given any remaining first-class seats. The rest of the players sat in coach class, and all of the coaches and managers sat at the back, in the smallest seats, and were the last to get off the plane.

This wasn't only important because it ensured the taller and older players had a comfortable plane ride—it also created an environment within the team of respect and servant leadership. He was introducing rituals that would propagate that attitude automatically.

He always put the team first, and this was the foundation of the legendary teams he coached and created. There is something here for all leaders, and especially those who want to build their team and expand their "we." Smith repeatedly made the least important people in the room (or the plane) feel the most important, and not because he wanted to indulge them but because he believed fervently in equality through servanthood. He did not take credit for the good, even when credit was due, but was the first to take credit for the bad: "If you do what we ask you to do, the victories will belong to you, and the losses to me." The former coach of North Carolina didn't demand respect; he humbly earned it.

Coach Smith's sincere belief that he wasn't the most relevant person in the equation is precisely what made him a stronger, more effective leader.

Around the time Dean Smith died, in 2015, *Forbes* published an article that talked about the death of heroic leadership.[30] Only, in that instance, they were referencing the industrial-era model that draws a clear, clean line between chief executives and employees. There is one person influencing progress and rewarding those who do his bidding; change comes about solely based on the actions taken by the heroic leader, either through inspiration, motivation, or removal.

It strikes me that this is an antiquated management model. The military-industrial culture of the 1950s and 1960s corporate America is gone, as is a large part of the manufacturing base of our economy, now offshore. At least two other things have occurred that have necessitated a change in corporate leadership culture.

First, most of our employers in the U.S. are now service organizations, so the product generated necessarily comes from a creative and closely engaged workforce; and second, our digital information systems allow for widespread and simultaneous dispersion of information, thus flattened organizations, making the command and control process of the old hierarchical structure nonfunctional and even rendering companies with such a structure inefficient dinosaurs, or at best, sloth-like.

If you've been paying attention, it will come as no surprise to you that I don't ascribe to this command and control model of executive management. I'm no hero, especially not in the way that *Forbes* describes heroism. And we all know by now that I don't consider myself an expert in any field. I could not have carried Sonic any more than I could carry a bus, and I depended heavily on those around me to take up a mantle of shared leadership. Together is how we carry the bus.

The thing is, I didn't really have an option when it comes to operating under a shared leadership model, because Sonic was and is a franchise business. Consistently and always, our franchisees have to buy in on everything, so we include them on virtually everything, from new product development to promotions to new technology initiatives. The strength of this shared leadership within our franchise system is one of the greatest strengths of Sonic. As they succeed, so does Sonic, which means their voices are critical.

I remember at one point in the mid-nineties, Sonic wanted to implement changes on the national level for consistent menus, consistent uniforms, awareness of customer feedback, and the need for capital investment at the store level. We felt like our younger and more market-based franchisees were more ready for the greater change than our older, multiunit owners. Instead of trying to drive a different viewpoint into our multiunit owners, instead of resorting to a steamroll approach, we began holding regional meetings where everyone was invited and included—the younger operators with the older owners. We didn't know how it would go, how everything we brought forth would be received, but we respected the members of the national Sonic family enough to present the information and ideas we had, and then open the floor for discussion. We called this process Sonic 2000, aiming toward the new millennium.

What happened next was inspiring to watch. These

younger operators provided a voice that we as corporate executives could not. They had perspectives we couldn't offer, as well as influence and relational capital that we did not have. And it was their voices, not ours, that caused our multiunit operators to change their viewpoint, so that everyone moved toward greater consistency across the entire system. This was a highly orchestrated process occurring over a number of months, and all stemmed from a teamwork approach.

And you know what? It was successful, even transformative. Instead of those in headquarters demanding things, we purposefully placed ourselves in the background, acknowledging we weren't the be-all and end-all source of information; we trusted our franchisees to make decisions that were in the best interest of the company as a whole. We provided a forum where an array of influential voices could prevail, and everyone moved along together. What a huge success for our company, operationally, sure, but also as a culture. It brought us closer together, helped to emphasize the shared leadership we believe in, and strengthened the brand—a win all around.

Often the first step is admitting you don't know everything.

Have you heard the old adage "What you don't know can't hurt you"? That long-used saying can actually be traced back to 1576 when author George Pettie wrote in *Petit Palace*: "So long as I know it not, it hurteth mee not." I used the saying plenty of times (mainly in regard to anniversary surprises for my wife or staving off my kids' curiosity about

Santa Claus), that is, until I realized how untrue it was. As it turns out, what you don't know can be more relevant than what you do know.

Take this, for example: in the 1950s, civil engineers unwittingly caused an increase in a debilitating waterborne infection called schistosomiasis, the second most common human parasitic disease after malaria. Its acute form is sometimes referred to as "snail fever" since the infection is most commonly found in areas with water that's contaminated with freshwater snails, the intermediate host for the parasites.

The civil engineers were just doing their job. When it came to irrigation schemes (like lifting water by pumps from rivers), they were schooled in the design, infrastructure, construction, and maintenance of such systems. They worked under the assumption that they just needed to know about concrete, water flows, impellers, casing, and pipes—and not about how to restrict velocities to prevent the snail species that carried the disease from multiplying. Their expertise in one area left them deficient.

The spread of schistosomiasis continued until eventually the U.N. was compelled to publish the simple guidelines for building the proper control mechanisms into the irrigation schemes.

Do you only seek the information and advice you *think* you need, as opposed to what you *actually* need to meet your own (or your organization's) goals? Do you make decisions based on what you know to be true, or do you purposefully seek to uncover the truths that could still be out there?

• • •

A MAN BY the name of Captain William Swenson was recently awarded the congressional Medal of Honor, the highest and most prestigious personal military decoration of the United States armed forces. Dating all the way back to 1863, it's awarded by the president in the name of the U.S. Congress and given to military service members who have distinguished themselves by acts of valor.

In 2009, Captain Swenson was stationed in Afghanistan and part of an operation to connect a group of Afghan government officials with native elders. When their column came under ambush, surrounded on three sides by as many as sixty insurgent fighters, Captain Swenson called for air support, and then repeatedly crossed fifty meters of open space under direct enemy fire to rescue the wounded and pull out the dead. Back and forth through the enemy's "kill zone" he went, carrying wounded comrades to a helicopter for medical evacuation. The six-hour firefight caused fifteen coalition deaths, and Swenson's actions are believed to have directly contributed to saving more than a dozen lives.

There's no question his actions were the mark of a courageous and committed leader, but here's the part I find most remarkable: By sheer coincidence, one of the medevac medics was wearing a GoPro camera on his helmet. His footage from that day shows Captain Swenson helping to carry a wounded soldier who had received a gunshot to the neck. They put him in the helicopter, and then you see Swenson bend over and kiss his forehead before returning to battle to rescue more.

Do you work with people like that? People who would put your safety before theirs? Who would express such tenderness and love to you in a moment of despair?

In the military, they give medals to people who are willing to sacrifice themselves so that others may gain. In business, we give bonuses to people who are willing to sacrifice others' well-being or performance so that we may gain. Can we all agree that we have it backward?

When my children were young, I remember being told that there was one quest in childhood, one that satiates the eternal question from a yearning deep inside: Do you *see* me? Our children spend their boundless energy in childhood vying for our affections and attention, all in the hopes of not being overlooked. But as our children grow older, the yearning to be noticed becomes contagious, spreads from the children to us, their parents.

The question "Do you see me?" is really about relevance. It's not a question of being seen, but a question of "Do I matter to you?"

In one of his TED Talks, motivational speaker and author Simon Sinek talked about meeting a barista named Noah at a coffee bar in the lobby of a Four Seasons hotel. After some enjoyable banter, Simon asked Noah if he liked his job. Without skipping a beat, Noah said, "I love my job!"

Knowing the distinct difference between liking something and loving something, Sinek asked him what the Four Seasons was doing that made him so genuinely enthusiastic about his job. Noah said that throughout the day, managers walk past him and ask how he's doing. How *he's* doing, not how the coffee bar is doing. And not just *his* manager, *any* manager. He then told Sinek how he also works at Caesars Palace and their managers walk past their employees to make sure they're doing everything right, like they're trying to catch them doing something wrong. On his shifts there, Noah just keeps his head down, stays under the radar, finishes the day, and cashes his paycheck. Whereas at the Four Seasons, he feels like he can be himself.

Can you imagine the different customer service experience you'd get from the employees at the two different hotels? Sinek was sure he wouldn't have gotten the same Noah at one as at the other. And it's not because of the employee, it's because of the leaders. Leaders are responsible for creating an environment in which people feel safe to be their best selves all the time. It trickles down from the top, that sense of camaraderie and true concern for one's well-being.

There are plenty of people at the senior-most levels of organizations who are absolutely not leaders. They are authorities, and people do what they say only because of the direct authority they have over them. But if given the choice, not many would willingly follow. On the flipside, there are plenty of people who hold no formal superiority—managerial, societal, or otherwise—who are leaders because, first and foremost, they refused to succumb to the supposed irrelevance placed on their lack of "position."

Richard Montañez grew up in a migrant labor camp—a makeshift settlement for hundreds of Mexican families trying to make a better life—in Southern California in the early sixties. He never made it past fifth grade, instead opting to work odd jobs in order to help support his parents and eleven siblings. In his teens, he got a job as a janitor at a local Frito-Lay plant where he mopped the floors, took out the trash, and stocked the bathrooms.

One day he saw a company-wide video of the CEO saying, "We want every worker in this company to act like an owner. Make a difference. You belong to this company, so make it better." The message stuck with Montañez.

Sometime later, he watched a street vendor in his neighborhood make elote—grilled Mexican street corn that's covered in cheese, butter, lime, and chili—and wondered what would happen if he took the same concept and applied it to a Cheeto, one of the main staples of Frito-Lay. So he tried it out, creating a variance of the elote recipe and putting it on Cheetos that had yet to be dusted with their orange flavoring. It was a big hit with his family and friends.

Remembering the CEO's earlier statements about acting like an owner with a stake in the company, and believing wholeheartedly that he meant them, Montañez called the CEO. That's right: he just picked up the phone and announced to the secretary on the other end of the line that he was the janitor at one of the California plants and that he had an idea he wanted to run by the boss. Not only did the CEO get on the phone to hear Montañez's idea, but he proceeded to invite him to pitch the idea in a couple weeks' time to a room of Frito-Lay executives.

Montañez purchased a three-dollar tie, had his wife help him prepare a presentation using a marketing book from the local library, and even drew a mockup of what the bag could look like. He went into the meeting with his head held high and won over the room, resulting in the creation of a new line of Frito-Lay spicy snack food, with Flamin' Hot Cheetos as its flagship product.

Montañez has gone on to fulfill several positions within the company, even becoming an executive himself, as well as a sought-after speaker, author, and subject of a film. While his tenacity and courage are remarkable, and he very clearly took initiative to create his own success, what's equally as extraordinary are the actions of the CEO.

As the top leader of the organization, the CEO placed no value on the "rank" of who was on the other end of the phone. He talked the talk of inclusivity, and when presented with the opportunity for consistent behavior, he walked the walk. He didn't tell his secretary to take a message. He didn't begrudgingly take the call to keep up appearances. He didn't take the idea and pitch it on behalf of Montañez, or even worse, pitch it as his own. He considered his job in the company to be one of service—to both the employees and the customers—so he didn't think twice about sitting in the back of the (metaphorical) plane.

What if we're all not as relevant as we think we are? Like in the case of the Frito-Lay CEO, what if we all realized that the height of our placement is reliant on the countless others holding us up?

Or, what if we're more relevant than we think we are? Like in the case of Richard Montañez, what if the playing field actually is level and the act of rising is reliant on how high we think we deserve to go?

What if both are true?

RULE OF THUMB #8:
A Win-Win Approach Is the Only Way to Sustain Growth.

Ultimately, utilizing this win-win approach, we took our business in the last decade to a completely different level, economically and geographically.

By 2011, the Great Recession had bottomed out and stabilized for most of us, including Sonic. We needed something, however, to charge our business and take it to a new level. We found the answer on several fronts, but on one avenue in particular.

For thirty years, as we had grown our marketing programs, we had always sold our operators on the benefit of the impact of local media. By 2010, however, national cable was playing such a significant role that we could focus all of our media expenditures there and, with no increase in expenditures, have significantly greater media presence in every single market in which we operated. The only thing this required was to convince our longtime operators in core markets to give up control of local marketing expenditures and locally budgeted media.

This was no small give. It required a two-thirds systemwide approval under our license agreements, but it also required our largest markets to forgo unique or peculiar expenditures in their local markets, to which they had become accustomed (even if sometimes of questionable impact).

It also required our individual operators to trust that our media predictions were correct, which was somewhat challenging coming out of the damaging years of the Great Recession.

But we took a complete win-win approach to this discussion, initiating meetings with our operators in June 2012 and campaigning throughout the system all summer through our September 2012 annual convention. At that convention, we surpassed the two-thirds approval level and went on to receive 90 percent approval.

And with this, with no increase in marketing expenditures, every single market in our system achieved at least a 20 percent increase in gross rating points (a broadly accepted media measurement applicable by market and in the aggregate).

This relinquishment of local power and control, for the greater good, was huge. Everyone came out ahead. It set our business on a consistent sales and profit growth path for 2013 through 2016. And it secured national awareness for our brand with American consumers.

I'm sure you've heard the saying and can fill in the blank: "You're only as good as your last _____." If you're an entrepreneur, you're only as good as your last start-up. If you're a chef, you're only as good as your last meal. If you're an actor, your last movie. An athlete, your last game. There's a pressure not only to keep churning out achievement after achievement, success after success, but also to keep topping ourselves. But the reality? The saying isn't true and the pressure isn't necessary.

These days it's easy to swallow the line that we're in a race against time—that we have to strike while the iron is hot. We want—or should I say, we feel—that we need to achieve something right now, and then want proper recognition to immediately follow. After all, we're only as good as the last thing that brought us accolades, right?

There's certainly nothing wrong with wanting to get better, but long-term growth truly is a journey, not a flash in the pan, even though our modern technological society makes it seem like we should take a win-now approach as opposed to a win-win.

There's a vast distinction there because win-now is individualized—an "I'm going to get mine" mentality. In that mindset, it's easy to lose sight of the fact that timeliness (which is interchangeable here with relevance) is significant but not as significant as timelessness. If we aim to be timeless—that is, enduring and consistent—the focus will automatically shift from self to others, from what it can offer you to what it can offer everyone.

Life

We live in an age of the "self"—self-improvement, self-help, self-preservation, self-care, self-made. On one hand, unprecedented good has come from the "self" epidemic, in both the personal and societal sense. Over the past couple decades, progress in the realms of exercise, addiction, and diet combined with advancements in modern medicine have made human longevity one of the greatest achievements of the modern era. But on the other hand, the focus on self seems to have morphed from a reasonable strategy of personal growth into an obsession with self-satisfaction and entitlement. Put another way, it seems like many people now prefer mirrors over windows.

When we look in a mirror, we see ourselves. We see a reflection of our pluses and minuses, and get an immediate recap of what we're presenting to the world. When we look out a window, we see everything else—other people, the state of our environment, and the inevitability of change, just to name a few. Mirrors cater to our ego and windows shift the focus to anything but.

Which are you more likely to do: look in a mirror or look out a window? Are you consumed with yourself and your needs, or are you more apt to look out for the well-being of others? Do you care more about your projection or your impact? The ultimate question becomes: in this self-obsessed world, are you going to fill your home with floor-to-ceiling mirrors or windows?

Work

In every movie or TV show that features an interrogation room, there's always a one-way mirror on one of the walls. The person being interviewed sees their reflection, but the FBI agents, police captains, or lawyers who are on the other side see through a transparent window. Which side would you rather be on?

When it comes to work, we're often in our office and focused on ourselves. We're inundated with emails, to-dos, paperwork, and agendas that will have a bearing on the success of our projects, deadlines, reputation, and annual review. So we toil away on our own job in our own little world, oblivious to the fact that our coworkers are like the agents in the other room—they can see more than we think they can. They can see through our attitudes and our words, our excuses and our deprecation. Ultimately, they can see how hard we're working for ourselves.

Is that what your coworkers are seeing when they observe you? If you're of the position of win-for-me versus win-win, they can see it. You may think you look fine in the mirror, but that mirror is transparent. That said, since it's transparent, they can also see if you're of the win-win posture; they can see those attributes playing out just as easily.

Think about those certain colleagues whom you can see through, the ones who are all about themselves. They're not fooling you. Do you want them on your team? Not really. Do you want to go out of your way to help them? Probably not. Would you be able to tell if they had a change of heart and prioritized the team over themselves? Yes. And seeing that, knowing it was for real, would permanently change the way you see and interact with them.

Leadership

When it comes to leadership, the difference between timeliness and timelessness is not insignificant, though the emphasis is now more on the difference between position and posture. Your position is your *what*. As in, what are you? You're the VP, the CEO, the head of a department. What you are is important and hard-earned. But your posture is your *how*, which is more important and harder to earn. It's how you carry yourself, how you lead those who answer to you, and how you'll ultimately get to where you want to go.

The positional leader takes the "you're only as good as your last _____" mentality as opposed to the posture of "everybody has something to offer." Think back to my situation with the Sonic franchisee who was getting heat from our corporate officers about his ice-cream program. That actually wasn't timely. As the CEO, if I were all about relevance, all about timeliness, then selling ice cream was irrelevant. Ice cream wasn't a staple of Sonic and didn't account for high annual sales; the thought of increasing those sales wasn't even on the radar of anyone at headquarters. But my posture was, and has always been, about leaning forward into new realms, looking ahead, knowing that progress is not win-now and it wouldn't serve us to disregard people or ideas as frivolous or meaningless. My posture was that it wasn't about the rungs of the ladder, it was about the ladder as a whole—where we were going and how best would we get there together.

I'm sure you're proud of your position, as you should be, but are you proud of your posture? Perhaps the better question is what's more important to you: furthering your position or strengthening your posture? A great leader cares more about the latter.

CHAPTER 9

Surviving the Perfect Storm

I've thrown a lot of different ideas at you in this book, in part because I'm trying to get you comfortable with the concepts of unpredictability and adaptability. As I learned in my thirty-five years with Sonic, and I hope you will come to see too, your path is limited to the options available. And most of these options aren't things of your choosing. And most of them, at first glance, won't align with your preferred path. And, sometimes, none of them will.

If you're going to embrace this life as a master of none, you simply must be okay with this potentiality. No, you have to be more than okay with it—you have to get to the place where you enjoy it, anticipate it, and allow yourself to thrive in unfamiliar environments, seizing opportunities you didn't even see coming. Adaptation is the foundation for success in work and in life.

Your ability to embrace unanticipated change will determine whether or not you survive the perfect storms that come up in your personal life and your career. If you have come to a place where you accept and learn to use change, perfect storms will drive you into new and exciting places you never could have gone before. But if you resist change, if you batten down the hatches and refuse to pull up your anchor, these perfect storms, when they arrive (and it's when, not if), will completely destroy you.

The first hint of my perfect storm came in December of 2017 when a major stockholder that owned 17 percent of Sonic started rattling our cages in a nonaggressive yet persistent way. Look at how low interest rates have gone, they argued, and look at how aggressive private equity firms have become in pricing companies. What they were actually saying was, "This could be a good opportunity for all of us to sell Sonic and make a lot of money." While I wasn't necessarily interested in selling Sonic to a private equity firm, I was the officer of a publicly traded company, and had a fiduciary duty at all times to consider the best interests of all of our shareholders.

Besides, look, they were correct, technically. It's fairly standard for companies to be valued and sold at seven to eight times the company's cash flow. Sometimes this number might reach ten, eleven, or twelve times cash flow. The number that would eventually be presented to us was fifteen and a half times cash flow, so this shareholder was on the money—

there was a high demand for solidly performing companies, and Sonic was one of them. The same stockholder kept insisting that we pursue this path, saying that, because money was almost free, we could potentially get a historically high price for Sonic. But they also wanted it to happen quickly, worried that changing market forces could eliminate this opportunity if we waited too long.

I understood what they were saying, but as someone with inside information into our own company, I saw things a little differently. I could see where they were coming from, but I understood the initiatives we had put into place, initiatives that I felt were about to greatly benefit our bottom line. I wasn't trying to stick a finger in their eye, but I also believed that within months we would be performing even better, and that would have a big impact on our sales growth, store performance, and stock valuation.

Now, publicly, this stockholder was being very nice, saying all the right things about the company. The statements they made were positive and supportive. Privately, they were getting rather persistent. But I felt the current price of the stock—and it was at around $28 per share at that point—was underperforming. So, in my mind, we had to get some of these initiatives on the fast track, while placating some stockholder concerns and trying to slow down a sale of the company.

When you're a leader, sometimes you can't take one position. Sometimes, it's a dance where you're both leading and following, speaking and inferring, waiting and pushing ahead. That was the case here. I needed to respond to the desire of our large stockholder, but I also wanted to see where our new initiatives were going to lead.

That stockholder was the first part of the perfect storm. Now, enter the second aspect of the perfect storm: a private equity group that was more than aware that we had an activist stockholder and began telling us that they wanted to purchase Sonic. Now, as an insider with thirty-four years in the company, I was hoping that if we timed everything properly, both parties would go away. I was hoping that the rising price would cause our "activist" stockholder to sell their own stock for a good profit, which would simultaneously intimidate the buyers, making them think this proposition had grown too expensive.

But then the third aspect of this perfect storm came into play: as our new initiatives gained momentum, we announced in June 2018 a great combination of (1) strong sales growth for the quarter ending with May, (2) the successful, initial stage systemwide rollout of our multiyear, technology-based, sales-driving initiatives, and (3) a new, three-year, $500 million stock buyback plan, our largest ever, by a long shot.

With this, our stock, which had been in the $20s in May, now hit $35 per share and my assumption was that the perfect storm had cleared. I even exercised all my "in the money" options, a move I would not have made had I seen what was coming next and a move that subsequently cost me a lot of money.

As the summer progressed, our activist stockholder grew quiet, as I had expected, but the interested private equity group did not. By August, they stated they would pay north of $40 per share for the company and in September they did just that, at $43.50 per share. We simply couldn't ignore it. Our board of directors honestly didn't have much of a choice. The offer was far beyond our stock's all-time high and, we felt certain, in the best interest of our stockholders to accept.

The funny thing is, this perfect storm came about outside my control or ability to plan for it. I didn't orchestrate or even initiate the sale, but all along I had been working hard to continually add value to the company. When you keep working hard, when you practice the principles we've been talking about as your regular course of action, extraordinary things can happen that you never imagined would. You just have to remain open to opportunities you didn't create.

There I was, in November 2018, standing in front of my staff, explaining that if the planned sale did go through, as it appeared to be likely, it was time for me to move on from Sonic, time to explore whatever was next, time to say "yes" to my next great adventure.

Many of us love the idea of change but find ourselves filled with anxiety when real change is on the horizon. We know what change necessitates: hard work. It was attributed to diplomat and three-time presidential candidate Adlai Stevenson that "change is inevitable, and change for the better is a full-time job." That's true, isn't it? We're going to change no matter what. Even if we try to embrace our current situation and try to lock it into place, change will break right through. Benjamin Franklin went further, stating, "When you are finished changing, you are finished." What we really need to do is accept that change is coming and then put in the hard work to ensure that the change we experience leads us to a better place.

We use a specific term all the time for owners or creators who have birthed something, raised it, and seen it mature—we call it their "baby." Right? Elon Musk, for example: Tesla is his baby. SpaceX is his baby. What we know of parenting, with that metaphor, is that your baby matures and ages and goes from being a toddler to a child to an adolescent and then eventually an adult. There comes a point, as a parent, where it's time to let your baby go out into the world by itself. You have to detach yourself from the decisions that are being made, that your grown child is now at liberty to make for himself.

Still a lot of entrepreneurs and business owners—and parents—have a hard time letting their baby grow into those new phases of maturation. They want to keep it under control, within their sphere of influence. They don't want it to leave the safety of their span of control or to develop a separate identity. This is understandable, of course—it takes an enormous amount of hard work, starting and building a company, and it's always difficult to walk away from that kind of emotional investment. But walking away usually becomes necessary.

There's a British entrepreneur named Tom Savage who founded and ran a handful of companies, ranging from tech-based start-ups to Ethiopian travel planning to grassroots marine conservation. For close to two decades, he secured millions of dollars from investors, employed hundreds of people, advised British Prime Minister Gordon Brown for the third sector, won social entrepreneurial awards, and oversaw the day-to-day operations of his different companies, which spanned five countries. Until one day he didn't. One day he came to the realization that he was a founder, not a CEO.

He walked away from his babies, not by force or in anger, but because he knew he wasn't the best fit for the job. The desire to control something he birthed wasn't as strong as the desire to see it properly flourish. He realized that spotting a problem and throwing all his energy into creating a company to fix it was his strong suit, not sitting at the helm of these companies and feeling beholden to customers, employees, regulations, investors, and others' expectations. How refreshing! In a world where people tend to hold on for dear life out of fear or a sense of obligation, very few exert such objectivity.

Do you?

I didn't start Sonic, but I was there from very early on. The founder's daughter, in one of the releases about my departure from Sonic, said that two men caused this concept to become what it was: her father, Troy Smith, birthed the company, and I came along and took it nationwide. It was a generous statement on her part, and it's true: I watched this company grow and grow and grow, and it felt, as this sale worked toward finality, that it was time for me to let it go, to let what once felt like my baby mature beyond me.

So, there I was, in the middle of a massive change. Sonic, the place I had worked for almost thirty-five years, was changing. My path was diverging from Sonic's. And it wasn't easy—I'm not here to tell you it was. Saying good-bye to longtime friends, to a brand I helped build, to franchisees I love like family, to a sales model my team developed through the years, well, it's all hard, and part of me resisted it. A part of me would have liked to keep this status quo going, sort of ease into this latter part of my life doing what I've always done at Sonic, with the comfort of walking on a path that's completely familiar to me.

But I know that wouldn't be the right thing to do. Sometimes saying yes means walking away from something you love.

It feels more than a little crazy writing that.

And yet, knowing my history as a master of none, it's not that surprising.

The other night, my wife and I were out to dinner and acquaintances were walking up to our table and thanking me. I guess they had made some money on the sale of Sonic. I had no idea they were stockholders—I just thought they were neighbors. This is just one of the rewards of living your life as a master of none.

• • •

I HAVE A ton of respect for leaders who embrace change, even more for those who can lead their teams through it. When a group of people can successfully navigate change, it's a kind of battle-testing that improves relationships, cooperation, and camaraderie. Change is one of the best team-building exercises on the planet.

One historical figure who experienced a monumental amount of change was Adlai E. Stevenson II. He's the one whose quote I mentioned earlier: "Change is inevitable, and change for the better is a full-time job." If General Patton is the measure of someone who never had to embrace change in his career, remaining a military man all his life, then Adlai Stevenson would be the complete opposite of that.

Stevenson came from a long line of influential people. His maternal great-grandfather, Jesse Fell, was a leading Republican during the nineteenth century, a huge supporter of Abraham Lincoln. His paternal grandfather, Adlai E. Stevenson, served as vice president once (under Grover Cleveland) and was nominated for the office a second time, alongside William Jennings Bryan. He also ran for the position of Illinois governor but was unsuccessful in his bid.

With those connections under his belt, he attended and graduated from Princeton, then failed out of Harvard Law School. He would eventually obtain a law degree from Northwestern University Law School and join a firm located in

Chicago. When the 1930s arrived, he began a thirty-five-year period of rapid career changes that would last until his death in 1965.

He entered public service in the early thirties, which became the only common thread that wove itself through the rest of his life. He began with the Chicago Council on Foreign Relations, and he became president of that organization in 1933. Once Prohibition was repealed in 1934, Stevenson became the chief attorney for FACA, the Federal Alcohol Control Administration. Late in the decade, he become one of the main voices of the Committee to Defend America by Aiding the Allies, a group that was lobbying for the United States to involve itself in World War II, if only by providing aid.

In 1940, he moved over into a Navy role, preparing speeches and representing the secretary of the navy on various committees. Once World War II ended, he worked for the State Department and helped with the formation and implementation of the United Nations. By the end of the forties, Stevenson was running for governor of Illinois (and winning).

When President Harry S. Truman decided not to pursue another term in 1952, he voiced his support for Stevenson. Stevenson wasn't interested in running for president, but he delivered the keynote address at the Democratic National Convention in Chicago, 1952, and when it came time for the party to select a nominee, they chose Stevenson, in spite of his hesitancy. He would end up running against, and losing to, Dwight D. Eisenhower, the incredibly well-known war hero. Stevenson ran again in 1956, but the political and economic climate was such that the country was content to keep Eisenhower in office.

When Kennedy won the presidency in 1960, Stevenson was given the opportunity to take on the position of U.S. ambassador to the United Nations, an opportunity he first declined, because he had his eye on the secretary of state position. But when Dean Rusk was named the new secretary of state, Stevenson eventually accepted. While at the United Nations, Stevenson served as president of the Security Council, advanced arms control, and did a lot to better the United States' relationship with newly formed African nations.

He died in 1965 in London, still the United States ambassador to the U.N., after speaking at the U.N. Economic and Social Council in Geneva only a few days before.

What a life. If anyone knew how to embrace change, Stevenson did, going from being a lawyer, to the president of a national organization, to a spokesperson, to the Navy during a world war, to presidential candidate, to U.N. ambassador.[31]

And not only did his career change—the world was in the midst of one of the more disruptive eras in history, and he survived two world wars, the Great Depression, the near nuclear holocaust of the Bay of Pigs, and even the turbulence of the sixties, which defined my own childhood. I can't help but wonder if living during such uncertain times makes it easier to embrace change.

One of the root words for "change" comes from the Greeks. In Greek mythology, Proteus is a sea god whose name suggests change, because he was able to change his shape as needed to escape capture. He could also foretell the future but would change his shape to avoid having to do so; he would answer only to someone who was capable of capturing him. From the story of Proteus comes the word "protean," with the general meaning of "versatile," "capable of assuming many forms with a positive meaning of flexibility, versatility, and adaptability."

In other words, change is courage. Like with Proteus (and Stevenson, for that matter), change can keep you from being trapped.

• • •

LEADING YOUR PEOPLE through change, modeling how it looks to embrace change as a "full-time job," is one of the most important responsibilities you have. If you reject or resist change in any way, your team will pick up on that, and an aversion to change will quickly become the norm, the way those around you operate. But if you can show them through example how to thrive in a changing environment, you'll be well on your way not only to becoming a master of none—you'll have an entire team of people ready to run with the concepts I've talked about in this book.

So how do you do that? How do you model this kind of countercultural love of change? In my opinion, the first trait is trust.

I believe a key to high-performing companies is employees who believe their leaders and managers to be highly trustworthy. If the organization you are part of doesn't trust you, if they're skeptical of your motives or ability or loyalty, navigating change is going to tear the team apart. But if you've put in the work to develop an environment of trust, where people are full of trust for one another, times of change will bring the team closer together. It will give you a kind of challenge that everyone can rally around, and when the change leads to what's perceived to be a win for the organization, you'll find yourself in an upward spiral of wins leading to wins. Trust is such a key element.

Another key component in successfully navigating change is having belief in the mission. There will be little motivation for your team to embrace change if they don't believe the change is going to advance them along the desired mission. But if they do, if they see the change as necessary to getting further along, that mission will fuel them through the change. This brings me back to the process I described earlier: What is the desired outcome? What is the process they intend to utilize in order to go down that road? Who is involved? Being able to answer these three questions at the onset of a major change event in the organization will increase people's belief in the mission, which in turn gives you a better chance to navigate the change successfully.

Another important aspect of getting through big changes is managing fear and staying energized. You know how it is—you set out on some kind of huge initiative, and three months in, six months in, a year in, everyone is getting exhausted, tired of working on the same old project, worried that all this hard work will be for nothing. This is one of the main reasons change is not easy to navigate—not because people resist something exciting in the beginning, but because often what started out as exciting turns into a drag. Fear and fatigue set in. But there is a way to manage this kind of stuff—you have to celebrate any little win that you can, and you need to tell stories about how people are making progress and how you are closing in on your goal.

A final word (or three) for those who want to successfully navigate change?

Discipline, discipline, discipline.

When you're working through a major transition or change, you have to keep everyone's eyes on the prize. You must do the things, day in and day out, that move you steadily onward. You have to make sure priorities are being adjusted so that the new thing is the most important thing.

These are all incredible ways to help your team, and yourself, embrace major changes.

• • •

YOU ARE ALIVE and evolving. Can you believe that? Are you able to fully appreciate what that means?

I am making plans now for my life's next chapter and, frankly, it's probably going to be the least structured time yet. Which shouldn't surprise you, coming from a master of none. My full intent is to leave things unstructured so that I can pursue any number of paths. I have people coming up to me with all kinds of suggestions: Why don't you do this? Why don't you do that?

Well, I want to put myself in a position where I can do anything I want to do. I want to put myself in a position where I can remain open to a number of different options and not lock myself into any of them. The lack of definition would probably make a lot of people nervous, but this is what invites freedom into my path and the kind of variety that gives life to my days.

RULE OF THUMB #9:
Embrace Options That Aren't of Your Own Choosing.

There's an old adage that goes like this: Change is good; you go first. It speaks to our love-hate relationship with any major shifts in our lives. We know we need it and yet we hold tight to this internal compass that resists it, even refusing to consider it at times. What if you learned to always consider change as an option? What if, even when doing the very thing you set out to do and doing it well, you still consider change? Do I sound like I'm out of my mind? Who would consider change when everything is working? I'll tell you:

those who know that quite often something good is the greatest enemy of something better.

Imagine if everyone stayed where they were for the sake of comfort or habit. Abraham Lincoln would have spent his life as a lawyer in Springfield, Illinois, instead of leading the nation through the American Civil War, abolishing slavery, strengthening the federal government, and modernizing the U.S. economy. Henry Ford would have been a farmer who ran a sawmill instead of becoming a captain of industry, a business magnate, and the founder of the Ford Motor Company. Michael Jordan would be known as a basketball player but not as a designer of Nike shoes, a spokesperson for Gatorade and Wheaties, an Olympic gold medalist, a professional baseball player, a movie star, and an owner of both an NBA team and an MLB team. Elon Musk would still be at PayPal, and SpaceX, Tesla, and SolarCity wouldn't exist. Rachael Ray would be the host of *30 Minute Meals* on her local CBS-TV affiliate in upstate New York and not an author of over twenty cookbooks, an Emmy-winning daytime talk show host, and the face of an empire that includes a magazine, pet food, and interior design collections.

What would have happened had those people not embraced the new opportunities that came their way? What if their fear of the unknown outweighed the promise of what could be? How different would their lives look—and in some cases, ours too—if they stayed where they were and settled for good instead of going for great? Now turn the tables. What have you not embraced that could significantly impact your world? What options and opportunities are waiting for you in the next phase of your life but first require that you forge ahead with a bold and blind faith?

Life

If you could make a change to your life right now, what would it be? Your schedule, your diet, your career? What's stopping you? Deep down, underneath all of your go-to justifications and excuses—time, money, energy, logistics—there's a very good chance your reservations are based on fear: fear of change, fear of uncertainty, fear of failure. Sound familiar?

In many ways, fear is a good thing. It's a fundamental, deeply wired reaction that protects us against perceived threats to our integrity or existence. The reaction starts in our brain and spreads through the body to make adjustments for the best defense, or flight reaction. These changes in our body prepare us to be more efficient in danger: the brain becomes hyperalert, pupils dilate, breathing accelerates. We go into an all-consuming survival mode with laser focus, which in turn makes other things unnoticeable. For example, if we're about to be involved in a car accident, we are focused wholly on the car hurtling toward us, our foot on the brake pedal, and our sharp turn of the steering wheel. We don't see the gas station to our right or the shopping mall to our left. We eliminate what we don't have to consider.

But you and I both know that fear isn't limited to

life-or-death situations. Fear emerges in all types of situations that don't warrant such an excessive reaction, and when we allow it to do so—that is, when we allow fear to take over when our survival isn't at stake—the result can be far more hindering that it is helpful. What is fear causing you not to consider? Are you holding yourself back from prospective opportunities? What options are available to you right now that you are resisting primarily because you don't want or feel ready for the change? Just think of all you could accomplish if fear wasn't in your repertoire.

Work

Being open to more options in your work setting can feel, on the one hand, disloyal, if you're considering work options outside your current job. On the other hand, considering all your options inside your current work environment can feel like the essence of being resourceful. The truth is that it might be a bit of both. Though I would never encourage anyone to be disloyal, I always understood when a team member at Sonic sought out something that was better for them outside the company. There is no rule that says you can only look for better options that improve the company you're working for.

The unspoken sentiment that exists in most corporate settings is that companies put money and resources into developing their employees and, in return, those companies expect devotion in the form of longevity. But at what cost? What if you're unhappy, undervalued, or overqualified in your current role? That's what makes the sentiment so archaic. There should always be an option to go find another job or go to another company; you should always be able to develop your career in the way you see fit.

Think about it from the employer's point of view. Let's say a professional football team signs you to a four-year contract worth tens of millions of dollars. Only a fraction of that is guaranteed and they can trade you any time. You sign the contract without batting an eye over those details because you know it's not personal, it's business. They're looking to form the best team they possibly can, and that may or may not include you in the long term. Why is the double standard acceptable? Why are they allowed to change their mind or go in another direction, but you're not?

I'm not telling you to quit your job. I'm telling you that the pressure you feel from your employer to stay put—whether it's subconscious or otherwise—could be keeping you from being open to a better opportunity. You're the captain of your own ship, and if you think you're going in the wrong direction, you have every right to change it.

Leadership

When was the last time you turned interruption on its head? The best leaders don't treat interruptions as troublesome;

they treat them as invitations to connect, to affirm, to reconsider. Douglas Conant, the former Campbell's Soup CEO, said that in his thirty-five years of leadership experience, he's learned that "thousands of little interruptions aren't keeping you from work, they *are* the work." Each opportunity is a chance to infuse someone else's day with meaning, he says. He calls them "touchpoints" and explains that every single interaction is rife with the potential to become the high point or the low point in someone's day. Every interruption offers an opportunity to lead impactfully, to set expectations, bring clarity to an issue, or infuse a problem with energy and insight.

As leaders, we should like more options. The real problems come when there are no alternative courses of action than the mediocre or questionable one before you. Turning interruptions on their head when they occur is a surefire way to ensure that more options remain available to you as a leader, and not just with the people you lead. Interruptions to your market strategy can be clues to an early trend. Interruptions to your sales strategy can give you a better sense of the nuanced needs in your customers. Interruptions to your perfectly scheduled day can help you remain flexible and open-minded when it comes to your priorities.

Being interruptible is the opposite of being distracted. It doesn't mean you don't focus on your work or obligations. It doesn't mean you don't take assignments and responsibilities seriously. It means that you don't assume that what you're doing is more important than what someone else needs from you. I don't know about you, but I'd rather be known for being open to occasional interruptions than the guy who never veers off task. The latter is what we expect of a robot. The former, an actual human being.

Which would you rather be?

EPILOGUE

Mastery Isn't Necessary to Live a Full Life

When my wife and I are being seated in the booth at our favorite restaurant, she will no longer let me sit in the window-facing seat. "I want you looking at me," she insists. After thirty-nine years of marriage she knows she's my top priority—but she also knows my mind is always wandering. And giving me the opportunity to stare out a window to see all the passersby can feel to her like she's sharing our date with countless others on the sidewalks of Oklahoma City.

What she doesn't understand—although I always try to explain it to her—is that having that stimulation makes me more capable of paying attention to her; the momentary diversion of people walking by actually allows me to stay more focused on my interactions with her.

In all areas of my life, the stimulation of more than one

activity keeps me energized on my primary activity. I can't do just one thing. On any given day, and particularly in my twenty-three years as CEO, I dealt with thirty different projects and topics, and that's exactly how I liked it. Contrary to how it may seem, the exorbitant number doesn't mean I'm doing a lackluster job on any of them, though I can see how one might think so—after all, the great assumption is that if everything is important, nothing is important. The fact that other things are going on around me, the fact that I'm always juggling, is what keeps me focused on the task at hand. It might be the same for you too and you don't even realize it.

The supposition that it's easier to focus when we're among distractions has been at the center of research for decades. Back in 1975, a psychologist by the name of Mihály Csíkszentmihályi recognized and named the psychological concept of "flow"—or being "in the zone," as it's sometimes called—and explained that it occurs when there's a perfect match between activity in brain networks involved in attention and the reward circuitry, which processes pleasure. When different networks synchronize their activity—like two pendulums swinging in time—it makes the business of thinking run a little more smoothly, which explains why this particular zone feels effortless when you're in it.

But even Csíkszentmihályi admits that it's not easy to achieve. In his book *Beyond Boredom and Anxiety*, he wrote, "Flow is difficult to maintain for any length of time without at least momentary interruptions." (And he said that well before smartphones came along and took what was left of our attention span.)

Those momentary interruptions piqued the curiosity of two cognitive neuroscientists who wanted to see if distractions were actually as hindering as everyone surmised them to be. Using brain imaging, they measured two different brain networks during the times their test subjects weren't thinking of anything in particular versus the times they were focused on one thing. They watched how the two fluctuated over time when people were asked to do a boring, repetitive task.[32]

Interestingly, they found the best way to sustain concentration wasn't to cut out the distractions altogether, but to allow them to carry on as a low-level background hum—essentially keeping our minds on a long leash and letting them wander a little before gently bringing them back to heel.

The regions of the brain that handle decision-making are still active when the conscious mind is distracted with a different task. That explains why Sir Isaac Newton was able to discover the law of universal gravitation while relaxing in the countryside instead of while working in his laboratory, and why you've had a great idea or an aha! moment while in the shower, driving your car, or chatting with a coworker.

A team at Columbia Business School wanted to test that phenomenon. Cognitive fixation, or spending too much time concentrating on our first ideas, hinders new ideas from being explored; they wondered if having a laser-sharp focus could backfire. What if distractions were what actually boosted our chances of finding truly novel solutions to our problems?

The team of researchers gathered together participants who had to think of as many uses as possible for specific common objects—in this case, a brick and a toothpick. One half of the participants had to do so in blocks, listing all the uses for the brick first before turning their full attention to the toothpick, while the others were told to alternate between the two tasks.

If immersed concentration is the key to creativity, you might have expected the first group to perform better, but that wasn't the case. From the sheer number of ideas they produced to the perceived novelty of the ideas, the multitaskers performed better. The lead researcher explained, "While they might have felt that they were on a roll, the reality was that without the breaks afforded by the continual task switching, their actual progress was limited."[33]

We're multifaceted beings who are capable of effective multitasking. And better still, that can be the key to our productivity! The same principle can be applied when talking about doing a great many things without mastering any of them. A diversity in interests and a wide range of knowledge and experience can be the very things that get you out from under the burden of focus and grant you a freedom you didn't know you needed.

Sometimes this lack of mastery comes in the form of an isolated decision. Sometimes it comes in an initiative that takes some time to implement. And sometimes lack of mastery feels like it extends through an entire period of time—this is how it felt during the Great Recession. I think a lot of us business leaders felt ill equipped to lead a business through that. The path was not clear at all. The future was one huge unknown.

At Sonic, we used it as a time to refine our operations, to bring some much-needed order to various parts of the business. We became even more consumer-driven, weaving together new initiatives so that sales eventually took off. During that time, we focused on things like enlarging and unifying the size of our hamburger patty, moving to all-beef hot dogs, returning to the "Two Guys" commercials, and reallocating our media dollars from a bunch of smaller local budgets to one larger, national budget. There wasn't a single decision we made that turned the massive ship, but the combination of many small decisions, led by many different individuals and teams, caused our business to take off.

I've said a lot of things throughout these pages that I hope you'll take to heart: embrace your wide variety of interests; don't give in to the prevailing pressure to spend all your time becoming an expert; be willing to drive innovation wherever you are; say yes; experience the broad swath of opportunities that life has to offer; embrace change as a way to navigate storms. You should know that little of it will come easily—you'll have to be intentional about most of these things, and you'll find yourself balking more than once as new opportunities present themselves. It takes courage, guts, and a serious side of "who cares what anyone else thinks" to live as a master of none. But the fact that we live in a distraction-heavy world with unlimited opportunities at our fingertips means endless adventures are ours for the taking.

Life doesn't need to trend toward rigidity and focus for us to be more successful and fulfilled. For work and life to continually flourish, we must let it remain an unpredictable, unspecified circus. The greatest lessons emerge from personal discovery, and variety is life's multiplier of opportunity.

Acknowledgments

This book is selective in telling the Sonic story. The stories included involve major steps in our progression, but also include mostly those elements that support a leadership theme I want to share. It does not detail some critical periods of our growth story, such as:

- The 1980s turnaround of our company-owned stores by Dennis Clark, and the simultaneous marketing oversight by Vern Stewart. This two-pronged turnaround saved the brand and our company, and made our 1991 IPO possible.
- The 1993–95 license renegotiation, which gave our franchisees term and radius protection, and gave us increased funding and up-to-date franchise powers, which in turn made all things possible thereafter. It was a bruising negotiation at the time but changed the path of our business.

- Our Franchise Advisory Council and its executive committee (Bobby Merritt, Buddy McClain, Chuck Harrison, Ted Kergan, Gary Kinslow, and James Junkin) for their years of collaboration, perseverance, and mutual respect.
- The 1990s marketing programs overseen by Pattye Moore and Scott Aylward, which, given our culture and history, were remarkable for what they achieved.
- The fifteen-plus-year role of Bill Fromm, Scott Aylward, and Kansas City–based Barkley & Evergreen. Their firm grew as much as ours, and no other firm played as critical a role in Sonic's growth.
- The Two Guys campaign, originally conceptualized by Brian Booker, Pat Piper, and Matt McKay, with its capacity for supporting any product, any daypart, and any time of the year. This was simply brilliant!
- The highly profitable negotiating skills of Drew Ritger successfully overseeing our systemwide purchasing programs from 1996 forward, and the franchise relations partnership he forged with Eddie Saroch, where they consistently produced great alignment with our franchisees and great results for our company.
- The 2012–15 role of James O'Reilly getting our sales and traffic moving again, with a leveraging punch

of national media, the return of the Two Guys, and a scream for ice cream!

- The gutsiness of our franchise leadership, time and again willing to support the centralized benefit of the brand over the narrow benefits of a single operator or single market. Their vote to "go national" with marketing dollars in 2012 changed the course of our business and cemented Sonic as a national brand in the consumer's eye.
- And, finally, the sustained dedication of our employees, officers, and franchisee leadership. So many worked so hard for so many years, their contributions are hard to isolate, but cannot be overstated!

And there are several individuals who deserve my overt thanks and special mention. "If I have seen further," Sir Isaac Newton famously said, "it is by standing upon the shoulders of giants." When it comes to my career, at least this much can be said. While my curiosity kept me in front of a wide range of people over the course of my life, there are a handful of giants who allowed me to stand on their shoulders and still others who I'm grateful to say were willing to walk alongside me for many years while we grew as individual leaders and learned from both shared experiences and one another's unique experience.

Leonard "Len" Lieberman joined our company's Board of Directors in 1988 when we restructured the ownership of our company. Our management team had bought the company in 1986 and restructured the ownership two years later because of an opportunity to buy out a capital partner who was ready to capitalize their gain and depart. Len joined our Board of Directors as a representative of our new New York–based, 51% partner. Len was the son of a Russian-Jewish immigrant; his family lived for some portion of his life in an apartment in Elizabeth, New Jersey, above the shop his father owned and ran, what we would now call a convenience store. Though his father was not literate and his mother died when he was fifteen, in a post–World War II environment, Len earned a degree in history at Yale, and later a law degree from Columbia Law School. In his professional career, Len spent a number of years in private law practice before becoming general counsel of a grocery chain known as Pathmark, for its parent company, Supermarkets General. His responsibilities grew over time such that he became CEO for several years before the company was purchased by a white knight in a hostile takeover in 1986. By this time, Len was fifty-seven years old. For the next twenty-two years, Len served on our Board of Directors and became a mentor and then friend of mine. During this time, he was a number-one advisor to me on most business matters, but was also a coach who could instruct me in private and leave those discussions private. He left our board just before turning eighty years old and remained a friend with whom I spoke weekly until his death in 2015. His widow gave me the honor of eulogizing him at his memorial service. I had met Len when I was a thirty-four-year-old general counsel, and he departed from my life when I was a sixty-year-old chairman and CEO. My indebtedness to him is significant, as was his contribution to the quality of my life.

Robert "Bob" Rosenberg joined our Board of Directors around 1993 and served for the next twenty-two or so years, as chair of our audit committee, then our compensation committee. He built the brand known as Dunkin' Donuts, for which he served as CEO for more than thirty years. Bob was absolutely instrumental in causing us to think about our company as a brand and insisting on a discipline that helped us build the same. His impact on our business was fundamental and positive and we built a different business because of him. Simultaneously with Bob's service to our company in the mid-1990s and his insistent questions about our brand, we begin utilizing the Kansas City advertising agency Barkley & Evergreen. Its chairman, Bill Fromm, also raised questions about brand and brand elements, and pushed us through our Sonic 2000 initiative to build a stronger and more profitable brand and company. These two individuals, Bob Rosenberg and Bill Fromm, did more to cause us to think differently about our business than anyone. Their impact on our company and my career was huge and positive. Each became my good friend, as well.

Frank Richardson was the president of Wesray Capital when we recapitalized our company with a Wesray affiliate in 1988. I owe Frank much due to this transaction, its contribution to my personal liquidity at the time and, simultaneously, an increase in my Sonic stock ownership (a multiple of eight times!).

I also owe Frank, Len, and Bob more than I can repay for their vote of confidence in elevating me to CEO in April 1995. This changed my path with Sonic—and changed my life!

Many of us owe thanks to my predecessor CEO at Sonic, Steve Lynn. He recognized both the need and opportunity to get Sonic franchisees working together, collaboratively. The job took unusual selling skills, which he possessed. And, as for me, he offered wide-open opportunities for business experience and executive leadership development. I may have been the greatest beneficiary of his leadership style during his eleven years with Sonic.

Bobby Merritt began his career with Sonic delivering bread to Sonic for a bread distributor. He liked what he saw and learned to manage a Sonic while still delivering bread. He eventually came to manage a single Sonic, a job from which he was eventually fired. Even still, he managed to become a franchisee in the 1970s and grew continuously through new store construction and acquisitions. Today, he owns 250 to 300 drive-ins and two of his three children are involved in his business. He must employ on the order of 10,000 people and have sales and rent revenues on the order of $350–$400 million. For fifteen years, Bobby served as chair of our franchise advisory council. There is hardly a franchisee with whom I worked more closely and cooperatively in my thirty-plus years with Sonic than Bobby. I came to consider him a friend and had a respectful and admiring relationship with him, his wife, Betty, and their kids. Bobby and I were able to work closely for decades and largely avoid significant conflict. I know there was much mutual respect and appreciation shared between us.

Buddy McClain became a single unit owner/operator after being fired as manager of a Sonic Drive-In. Before that, at age twenty, he worked the line at a rural Louisiana toilet seat manufacturing plant. Buddy reopened a single closed Sonic in Mississippi in the 1970s and today owns and operates a hundred-plus drive-ins in three states. His restaurant sales and rental revenues must now surpass $150 million. He is a very significant employer in his home of Jackson, Mississippi, and the state of Mississippi, flying his private aircraft between his geographic areas of business concentration. Buddy succeeded Bobby Merritt as chair of our franchise advisory council around 2015. He engages both daughters and his wife in his related businesses in Jackson. Buddy and I worked closely for many years and there were few operators I saw go through more change, development, maturation, and success than Buddy. Our relationship developed over time from one of pure business, through some "tough love" periods, to mutual respect and success.

The first two people I hired at Sonic were Bill Dyke in 1985 and Launa Ashby in 1986. Bill came to us as an attorney and Launa as a paralegal. They were capable, dedicated, and professional employees. When I announced my departure from the company in 2018, it was both poignant and impactful to see these same two folks as senior employees sitting in the meeting and soaking up the new developments. It was my honor and pleasure to work with both of them for more than thirty years.

My assistant of twenty-seven years, Renee Chapman, has experienced every peak and valley with me for most of her adult life! She has been a big part of all I have achieved, and her loyalty, support, and continuously innovative assistance leave me forever grateful.

My appreciation of Brent Cole is deep and wide, as he assisted in conceptualizing this book, as well as helping think it through, draft provisions, and provide continual review. He has been a pleasure to work with and a partner in this process in most every sense of the word.

There are others too numerous to mention, but here are a few: Gene Rainbolt for his forty years of multifaceted service to our founder, Troy Smith, and to me; Kathy Taylor for her Sonic board service, on-off-on again over a thirty-year period, for a long-standing friendship, and ever-present willingness to listen and offer wise advice; Larry Nichols for his board service and helping set straight elements of our board governance; Scott McLain for devising the pitch of our multilayered growth strategy; and many more!

Above all, my greatest love, thanks, and appreciation has to be reserved for my wife, Leslie, and our two sons, Stuart and Bennett.

As I have approached any endeavor, Leslie has been my constant advisor, supporter, and partner—perhaps, at times, even to her chagrin! Over the years, some folks might be surprised that my words of advice to them arose from thoughts originating with her, setting me on a better course, causing me to rethink a path. The post of a CEO can be a lonely one, but my journey was always softened by the knowledge that I had a partner who had my best interests at heart and knew how to impart perspective when my listening instincts weren't the best. As the Oklahoma songwriter Jimmy Webb offered to his lover in his lonesome tune "Wichita Lineman": "I need you more than want you, and I want you for all time."

When I joined Sonic, Leslie and I were twentysomethings with no kids. As I departed in 2018, our two sons were in their late twenties and early thirties, roughly as we had been a business life before. Our sons have been the richest additions to my life, offering perspective by pulling me away from self-centered thinking as a younger father, and offering joy and renewal as I observe them move on in their own life paths. They are both good people and good citizens, and offer me optimism that their generation will rise to meet life's demands with courage and commitment.

To my parents, I think of many things, but can distill it more succinctly at this point in life. My love of music, politics, and history comes from my parents, and colors my palette daily, even now. But it was their dogged perseverance that crept into me more quietly and deeply, more than most any other trait. Certainly they shared this trait and, if it wasn't in my DNA, it came in lessons learned by observation and insistence.

My family has been my foundation all these years; this cannot be overstated. To them I owe everything.

Notes

1 Gary Orfield, Christine Mattise, and Brian Willoughby, "BROWN V. BOARD: Timeline of School Integration in the U.S.," Teaching Tolerance, accessed January 6, 2020, https://www.tolerance.org/magazine/spring-2004/brown-v-board-timeline-of-school-integration-in-the-us.

2 Linda W. Reese, "Clara Luper (1923–2011)," accessed November 14, 2019, https://blackpast.org/aaw/luper-clara-1923.

3 "Bohanon, Luther Lee," in *Encyclopedia of Oklahoma History and Culture*, accessed January 6, 2020, http://www.okhistory.org/publications/enc/entry.php?entry=BO004.

4 History.com editors, "George S. Patton," History.com, November 9, 2009, https://www.history.com/topics/world-war-ii/george-smith-patton.

5 Louisa Sheward, Jennifer Hunt, Suzanne Hagen, Margaret Macleod, and Jane Ball, "The Relationship Between UK Hospital Nurse Staffing and Emotional Exhaustion and Job Dissatisfaction," *Journal of Nursing Management* 13,

no. 1 (2005): 51–60, https://doi.org/10.1111/j.13652834.2004.00460.x.

6 Jim Edwards, "Check Out the Insane Lengths Zappos Customer Service Reps Will Go To," *Business Insider*, January 9, 2012, http://www.businessinsider.com/zappos-customer-service-crm-2012-1.

7 Daniel Kreps, "Walter Becker, Steely Dan Co-Founder, Dead at 67," *Rolling Stone*, June 25, 2018, https://www.rollingstone.com/music/music-news/walter-becker-steely-dan-co-founder-dead-at-67–127755/.

8 Eddi Fiegel, *Dream a Little Dream of Me: The Life of "Mama" Cass Elliot* (London: Sidgwick & Jackson, 2005).

9 Fred Schruers, *Billy Joel: The Definitive Biography* (New York: Three Rivers Press, 2015), pp. 186, 187.

10 Sapna Maheshwari, "The Delicate Dance of a Progressive C.E.O. in the Trump Era," *New York Times*, January 15, 2018, https://www.nytimes.com/2018/01/15/business/media/sonic-drive-in-clifford-hudson.html.

11 "Mind the Workplace: Workplace Wellness Report" Mental Health America, accessed January 6, 2020, https://www.mhanational.org/research-reports/mind-workplace-workplace-wellness-report.

12 "20 Things Sir Richard Branson Has Done That Prove He's the Spirit of Adventure in Human Form," Mpora, accessed January 6, 2020, https://mpora.com/outdoors/outsiders/things-sir-richard-branson-done-prove-hes-spirit-adventure-human-form.

13 Ruth Umah, "Richard Branson Funded His First Business at 16 for Less than $2,000," CNBC, August 28, 2018, https://

www.cnbc.com/2018/08/28/richard-branson-launched-his-first-business-for-less-than-2000.html.

14 "Bob Kulhan," Business Improvisations, accessed January 6, 2020, http://businessimprov.com/instructors/bob-kulhan/.

15 Frank Thomas and Ollie Johnston, *Disney Animation: The Illusion of Life* (New York: Abbeville Press, 1984).

16 Adela C. Y. Lee and Silkroad Foundation, "Marco Polo and His Travels," accessed January 6, 2020, http://www.silkroadfoundation.org/artl/marcopolo.shtml.

17 "The Journeys of Marco Polo and Their Impact," Encyclopedia.com, December 27, 2019, https://www.encyclopedia.com/science/encyclopedias-almanacs-transcripts-and-maps/journeys-marco-polo-and-their-impact.

18 N. Eagle and A. Pentland, "Eigenbehaviors: Identifying Structure in Routine," Ubicomp '06, September 17–21, 2006, Orange County, CA.

19 Marc Ferro, *Nicholas II: Last of the Tsars* (New York: Oxford University Press, 1994).

20 Orlando Figes, *A People's Tragedy: The Russian Revolution* (London: Bodley Head, 2017).

21 "Harriet Williams Russell Strong," Wikipedia, December 23, 2019, https://en.wikipedia.org/wiki/Harriet_Williams_Russell_Strong.

22 Susan Fourtané, "51 Female Inventors and Their Inventions That Changed the World and Impacted the History in a Revolutionary Way," Interesting Engineering, February 27, 2019, https://interestingengineering.com/female-inventors-and-their-inventions-that-changed-the-world-and-impacted-the-history-in-a-revolutionary-way.

23 Joan Hibler, "Reed Hastings," Encyclopaedia Britannica, October 4, 2019, https://www.britannica.com/biography/Reed-Hastings.

24 Kinsey Grant, "Why Netflix CEO Reed Hastings Is a Genius," TheStreet, November 3, 2017, https://www.thestreet.com/story/14368670/1/why-netflix-ceo-reed-hastings-is-a-genius.html.

25 James Gill, "What's Next for Netflix? 12 Important Details We've Learned About the Future of On Demand," *Radio Times*, accessed January 6, 2020, https://www.radiotimes.com/news/2017-04-21/whats-next-for-netflix-12-important-details-weve-learned-about-the-future-of-on-demand/.

26 "10 of Benjamin Franklin's Lesser-Known Feats of Awesomeness," Mental Floss, January 17, 2018, http://mentalfloss.com/article/29762/10-ben-franklins-lesser-known-feats-awesomeness.

27 "Benjamin Franklin," Biography, Engineering and Technology History Wiki, accessed January 6, 2020, https://ethw.org/Benjamin_Franklin.

28 Nolan Moore, "10 Most Outrageous Things Benjamin Franklin Ever Did," Listverse, June 6, 2019, https://listverse.com/2014/11/20/10-most-outrageous-things-benjamin-franklin-ever-did/.

29 Michael Levy, "Dean Smith," Encyclopaedia Britannica, May 20, 2019, https://www.britannica.com/biography/Dean-Smith.

30 Carsten Tams, "Bye-Bye, Heroic Leadership. Here Comes Shared Leadership," *Forbes*, September 10, 2019, https://www.forbes.com/sites/carstentams/2018/03/09/bye

-bye-heroic-leadership-here-comes-shared-leadership /#583b41442c67.

31 "Adlai E. Stevenson," United States History, accessed January 6, 2020, https://www.u-s-history.com/pages/h1760.html.

32 Michael Esterman, Sarah K. Noonan, Monica Rosenberg, and Joseph DeGutis, "In the Zone or Zoning Out? Tracking Behavioral and Neural Fluctuations During Sustained Attention," *Cerebral Cortex* 23, no. 11 (November 2013): 2712–23, https://academic.oup.com/cercor/article /23/11/2712/303412.

33 Jackson G. Lu, Modupe Akinola, and Malia F. Mason, "'Switching On' Creativity: Task Switching Can Increase Creativity by Reducing Cognitive Fixation," *Organizational Behavior and Human Decision Processes*, 139 (March 2017): 63–75,https://www.sciencedirect.com/science/article/abs/pii /S074959781630108X.

Index

About the Author

CLIFFORD HUDSON is the former chairman and chief executive officer of Oklahoma City–based Sonic Corp. In the Clinton administration, he served as chairman of the board for the Securities Investor Protection Corporation. Cliff also served as a trustee of the Ford Foundation and is a past chairman of the board of the National Trust for Historic Preservation. He and his wife have two adult sons and divide their time between Oklahoma City and New York.